GET AWAY OLD MAN

WILLIAM SAROYAN

Get Away
Old Man

A Play in Two Acts

"For an old man he is old"

HARCOURT, BRACE AND COMPANY, NEW YORK

first edition

A WARTIME BOOK

*This complete edition is produced in full
compliance with the government's regu-
lations for conserving paper and other
essential materials.*

To

Walter Papazian

in memory of the great days
on the vineyard in the valley

NOTE

Get Away Old Man opened at the Cort Theatre on West 48th Street in New York City on Wednesday, November 24, 1943, produced and directed by George Abbott, in sets designed by John Root, with the following cast:

PATRICK HAMMER	Edward Begley
HARRY BIRD	Richard Widmark
ROSE SCHORNBLOOM	Hilda Vaughn
BEN MANHEIM	William Adams
SAM	Glenn Anders
CORRESPONDENT OF THE NEW YORK TIMES	Edwin Hodge
MARTHA HARPER	Beatrice Pearson
PIANIST	Sula Levitch
BETTY FITCH	Joyce Mathews
MESSENGER	Mason Adams
DOCTOR	Jerome Thor

The following note by me appeared in the program:

Get Away Old Man is an American play, and nothing else. It was conceived, written, and produced solely to entertain. All of its action is invented. All of its characters are imagined.

If any character in the play is based on any living person in the world, that person is myself. I don't know anybody else well enough to praise or criticize, celebrate or condemn, immortalize or damn.

The play was poorly received by the drama critics of the New York papers, and closed Saturday, December 4, after thirteen performances.

WILLIAM SAROYAN

New York
December 1, 1943

THE PEOPLE

HARRY BIRD, a writer
PATRICK HAMMER, a moving picture executive
BEN MANHEIM, his assistant
ROSE SCHORNBLOOM, manicurist to Mr. Hammer for 11 years
SAM, an acquaintance of Harry Bird's
MARTHA HARPER, a young woman
BETTY FITCH, a moving picture star
CORRESPONDENT FOR THE NEW YORK TIMES, a middle-aged man
PIANIST, a small man
MESSENGER, a young man
DOCTOR, a young man

THE PLACE: California

THE TIME: A day of the week

A large shabby second-floor room, formerly used as a photographic studio, with steps coming up. The center wall is covered with a fresco of a blue sky with white clouds. There is a small dressing room with a drape in the doorway. A circular platform with three steps. An electric box with a switch. A water jar with a container of paper cups. A number of pieces of gaudy furniture. A baby grand, electrically operated player piano. A blackboard on an easel, beside the piano. On the blackboard is printed: Who is Sam?

HARRY BIRD is standing in the middle of the room, throwing darts at a target on the wall, while the pianola is banging away at an old razzle-dazzle piece—perhaps "Hand Me Down My Walking Cane."

PATRICK HAMMER is seated on a divan with ROSE SCHORNBLOOM, who is manicuring his hands.

After throwing three darts, HARRY BIRD goes to the target, takes out the darts, goes to the pianola, shuts it off, puts the darts in a box on the circular platform, and walks idly to the couple on the divan. He looks at the man, then at the woman, then walks away, and suddenly begins to reach upward as far as he's able to.

HAMMER
What are you doing that for?

3

HARRY

I do this when I'm tired. See? Reach way up. High. Either this, or I jump.

HAMMER

Jump?

HARRY

That's right. I once jumped over a doctor who tried to tell me I ought to go to a hospital for a month—to rest. He was sitting at his desk at the time. I got up on a chair and jumped over him. That was seven years ago, when I was almost twenty. I've never been in a hospital in my life. I intend to live to be as old as you are. How old are you, Mr. Hammer?

HAMMER

I'll be sixty-three on Christmas Day.

HARRY

You mean to tell me you were born on Christmas Day?

HAMMER

Yes, I was.

HARRY

Amazing.
          (Pause)
Where?

HAMMER

Dublin.

HARRY

Are you from Dublin, *Ireland?*

HAMMER

I was born there, but my family moved to New York when I was eleven.

4

HARRY
        (Pause)
How often do you get a manicure?

HAMMER
Twice a week.

HARRY
        (Suddenly)
Well, what about it?

HAMMER
What about what?

HARRY
I think it's wonderful being visited by you and your manicurist,
and I like the way our conversations go, but—let's make up our
minds, one way or the other. I'm tired. I'm bored.

HAMMER
        (Courteously)
Now, Harry, don't get bored. Don't be impatient. I've told you
again and again, this is not an everyday matter. I want you to
get acquainted with me, and I want to try to get acquainted
with you. I've been in this business thirty-five years.

HARRY
That's too long— What do you do? You get your hands manicured. What's the matter with your hands? You don't need a
manicure. No offense to you, Miss. I suppose you get a good
tip when you manicure the hands of a man like Mr. Hammer.
Or maybe you feel proud to do it. Maybe you're satisfied to feel
proud and let the tip go.

ROSE
        (Confused)
My name is Rose Schornbloom.

5 .

HARRY

I'll make a note of that.

ROSE

And I'm satisfied to do my work as I'm called upon to do it, and to mind my own business.

HARRY

(Gently)
Don't be so proud of cleaning the hands of a corrupt man.

ROSE

(Excited)
Mr. Hammer is not a corrupt man.

(HAMMER smiles)

HARRY

(Idly)
You're a mother, not a manicurist. What do you think you're trying to do?

HAMMER

(Drawing his hand away)
What's the matter with you, Woman?

ROSE

I'm sorry, Mr. Hammer. I hope I didn't hurt you, but he makes me nervous.

HARRY

That's it, get nervous. Let him clean his own hands. Let him keep them clean.

HAMMER

Just a moment, Harry.

HARRY

All right, one way or the other. You asked me here, and you

can ask me to go. After three weeks, you may as well know I'm ready to go. I want to take a slow drive home, before it's too late.

HAMMER
Too late for what?

HARRY
Too late for me. You're sixty-three years old, born Christmas Day, but remember, I'm twenty-seven.

HAMMER
Harry, I've told you before, President Roosevelt himself has informed me—

HARRY
Listen, Mr. Hammer, you don't have to give me that big-man stuff. I know you're a big man in this country. That's fine, but it's got nothing to do with me. Now, what's on your mind?

HAMMER
I want you to write the greatest story ever written.
        (*Pause*)
Ave Maria!

HARRY
        (*Quietly*)
What the devil are you talking about?

HAMMER
I'm talking about a great story. America needs that story, as only you can write it. I want your great understanding, your sympathy, your compassion for little people, for soldiers, sailors, and marines.

HARRY
I never saw a soldier in my life.

HAMMER

That's what I mean, Harry. Your understanding for young men *dressed* like soldiers, sailors, and marines.

(*Piously*)

Ave—Maria!—the whole bleeding heart of humanity—while beautiful airplanes destroy great cities—cities made of human spit and pain, every one of them the holy home of life, destroyed overnight in evil darkness—Ave Maria, Harry, while whole nations change or die—brotherhood smashed, family torn apart, and the dream of life broken like a cup struck by a hammer—

HARRY

Yeah, and that's your *name*—Hammer.

HAMMER

(*Swiftly*)

—The dream of life broken like an egg dropped from a trembling hand. Ave Maria, Harry, while the mothers of life weep and pray, and the fathers of men rock in silence with shame and grief.

(*Pause*)

The whole world's gone mad and no man knows who's innocent or guilty. That's the story, Harry, and you've got to write it for me. Ave Maria, while each of us is murdered, while each of us murders his brother. Ave Maria, Harry, while—

(*Pause. He looks at his hand being manicured*)

HARRY

(*Interrupting*)

—You get your claws trimmed, and I watch, and worry about Rose.

(To ROSE)

Get yourself with child. Mr. Hammer needs him for the great epic he's just written.

ROSE

(*Softly but with terrible rage*)

I don't know who you are, but whoever you are—I think you

8

ought to know I am a mother. I have four children. I have a
son almost as old as you are, in the Army.

HARRY
> (Gently)

Then you married the wrong man. Who did you marry?

ROSE
You go to hell. If you can be vulgar, so can I. You go to hell,
you—you—

HARRY
I'm sorry you married the wrong man. I'm sorry you had the
wrong children.

ROSE
The wrong children?

HARRY
You never saw your kids the way they are. You won't mind at
all if the soldier's killed, because he was a mistake in the first
place. The whole thing was a mistake. Your children, as well as
the war.

ROSE
> (Standing, to HAMMER)

Every mother feels her children aren't the right ones—the ones
she really wanted, the ones she always loved, even before they
were born. It's only evil rudeness to tell a mother such a thing.
> (She turns and runs down the steps, out of the office)

HARRY
I'm disgusted with myself.

HAMMER
No, Harry! That's what I want. That's exactly what I want. Ave
Maria! The story of women—all women—the story of mother.
We'll give the human race a new birth.

9

HARRY

You've been talking to Ben Manheim. Well, he doesn't know the war's over. He's a great man, one of the few people I've met out here who doesn't make me sick to my stomach, but he's a fool, too. He's been trying for twenty years to be a Saint, and you won't let him. Why don't you let the man be a Saint? You'll make more money than ever. He's so backward and noble he doesn't know the war's over.

HAMMER

But the war *isn't* over.

HARRY

Don't be a dreamer, the war's over.

HAMMER

Well, sometimes I can't follow you, Harry, but I know your heart's in the right place, I know you can write, and I know you're a genius.

HARRY

That's a lot of hooey. I didn't need to hurt that poor woman. Give me her address and I'll send her some flowers.

HAMMER

I'll send her some.

HARRY

(*Earnestly*)

Will you? Thanks. I'll pay for them, but put your name on the card. You mean a lot to her. Send her some candy, too, and some books. Don't send her any of my books. She'll buy those herself—and read them secretly. She'll love them, too. When are you going to read a book?

HAMMER

Now, Harry, I haven't time to read. But I promise you this— if you write Ave Maria for me, I'll read it.

HARRY

Thanks. That's a mighty tempting offer.
(Pause)
I wouldn't work for anybody.

HAMMER

But if you come into this organization, you've got to work for somebody.

HARRY

Who, for instance?

HAMMER

Me. I'm not so bad. I think I understand you. I believe I even like you. I've heard not many people do, but I believe I am telling you the truth when I tell you I like you. I know this business, and I know when I've run into a real writer. Write Ave Maria for me. I'll pay you anything you like—anything at all.

HARRY

What the hell's happened to you, anyway? Why do those words mean so much to you? What are you driving at?

HAMMER

I admit I've not lived a blameless life, or that I live a blameless life now, but I would like to live a blameless life.

HARRY

Then do it. Why don't you do it?
(Pause)
Because you're a crook.

HAMMER

I know, I know. If you insist, I'll admit I'm a crook. Or what you call a crook. But who isn't? You can't survive in this world and live like a decent human being, that's all. You can't! I'll go to my knees like this, reverently, to any man who can do it. It's too easy to say I'm a crook, because I'm more than that—a

11

damn sight more. You don't want to write Ave Maria because you know it means a lot to me—*personally*—and you're right. Sure it means a lot to me.

HARRY

Why?

HAMMER

(*Confused*)
Why? I'll tell you why.
(*Suddenly angry*)
I've got a lot of respect for you, young man, but I can be tough too, and I can tell you to your face that I think you're a gutter boy—and you'll never leave the God damn gutter, because it made you. You only looked up and found the stars, you didn't put them there.
(*Pause, gently*)
I wouldn't talk this way to my own sons—three great big half-wits, breaking their necks trying to be big men. Big men! You told the poor manicurist the truth, and you told me the truth, too. My sons are the sons of some idiot I don't know, and if any man in the world is truly my son, it's you, Harry, and I tell you you're a tough gutter boy who would knife me in two minutes if you could.

HARRY

You're a great actor.

HAMMER

The greatest in this business, but I'm not acting now. You haven't seen me act. I'm not laughing in my heart the way I do when I'm teaching some fatheaded actor or actress a thing or two. I've gotten old. I've never known until now how old I've gotten. It makes me cry—all the time. Write the story for me. You're my son, and I'm an old man.
(*Pause*)
Now, how about it?

12

HARRY

    Get away, old man!
        (He goes to the stairway)

HAMMER

        (Leaping)
    You're a guttersnipe! You're a common guttersnipe!

HARRY

    When you're ready to be honest with me, pay me another visit.
        (He goes. HAMMER *lifts the telephone receiver, dials a number)*

HAMMER

    Ben? Come right over to Harry Bird's office, will you?
        (He hangs up, and for a moment studies his left hand and three unmanicured fingers. He starts the pianola. After a moment or two BEN MANHEIM, *a man almost as old as* HAMMER, *comes up the stairs. There is something shy and great about this man, who is nothing but a plain happy man with a home, a library, an expensive phonograph, many albums of music, a wife, and two children. There is even something youthful about him, a kind of concern and eagerness about all sorts of unimportant things, a generosity for them, and a humor concerning the surprises people get from one another. He scarcely glances at his old friend, and yet he knows* HAMMER *is both surprised and irritated, perhaps shocked. He remains standing, waiting for* HAMMER *to acknowledge his presence.* HAMMER *turns off the pianola. Suddenly)*

Ben, what about this son of a bitch? The more I get to know him the less I understand him. A few minutes ago I thought he and I were going to be great friends—father and son almost—and do you know what he told me?

MANHEIM

    If you'll tell me what you told him, I think I can guess what he told you.

HAMMER

Do you really think you know him?

MANHEIM

Well, maybe not. What did you tell him?

HAMMER

I told him to write my story—and I'd pay him anything he liked. I told him—well—I told him he was my son, if any man in the world was.

MANHEIM

He knew you weren't telling the truth, boss.

HAMMER

(Swiftly, with anger)

Just a moment, Ben. You know things I don't know and you understand things I don't understand. But don't be so sure of yourself all the time. How do you know I wasn't telling the truth? It so happens I was.

MANHEIM

I'm sorry, boss.

HAMMER

And never mind calling me boss all the time. You've known me long enough to call me by my name.

MANHEIM

It's been a long time since you've wanted me to call you by your name, but I'll do it until you ask me not to.

HAMMER

(Gently)

From now on, Ben, when we're alone please be good enough to call me by my name.

MANHEIM

(Smiling)

14

All right, Patrick.

(HAMMER *looks at* MANHEIM)

HAMMER

Now, tell me about this maniac. Why can't I get along with
him?

MANHEIM

I'm afraid he doesn't trust you.

HAMMER

So what? What if he doesn't trust me? He's a crook himself,
I'm an amateur beside him. I don't say he can't write, but be-
sides being able to write, the son of a bitch understands things.
He's from the streets. Writers ought to come from good homes.
From pleasant people who respect one another, who believe in
the things everybody else believes in. For three weeks I've
dropped everything for him, but it just doesn't seem to work.
    (Pause)
Ben, do you think I ought to forget the whole thing?

MANHEIM

Yes, Patrick, I honestly think you should.

HAMMER

Why?

MANHEIM

Because he'll make trouble.

HAMMER

    (Reflecting)
Yes, I think you're right. I'll forget the whole thing. It's too
much for me. I'm too old, and he's too young. And too swift.
What makes him so swift?

MANHEIM

Being right, I suppose.

15

HAMMER
Am I slow?

MANHEIM
No, Patrick, you're still swifter than anybody else I know.

HAMMER
Am I wrong?

MANHEIM
No.

HAMMER
I'm right?

MANHEIM
Not quite, but not *wrong*, either. He's just right.

HAMMER
(*Furious*)
How the hell do you know?

MANHEIM
Well, Patrick, if he isn't right, whoever writes his books is. He
has a way of throwing you off, misleading you, confusing you—
he does it to get everything more deeply right than it would be
otherwise. And I guess he does it to be amusing.

HAMMER
Amusing to *who*? He's not amusing to me. He's vulgar, he's
unkind, he talks around in circles, he jumps from one thing to
another. I don't find him amusing at all. Who's he amusing to?

MANHEIM
To a number of people who move around with him.

HAMMER
What people? I've never seen him, except he was alone. He's
got no business manager, no agent, no friend. What people?

MANHEIM
Mostly dead people.

HAMMER
Ben, what the hell are you talking about?

MANHEIM
Well, to begin with, you'll remember I urged you not to get him to come here. I didn't want him to come here for *his* sake as well as for yours. And mine, too, for that matter. But you insisted. I knew he'd make trouble. The son of a bitch, as you call him, has made trouble everywhere he's gone. I was pretty sure he'd be the way he is, and that way isn't comfortable for any of us. Two weeks ago I handed him the story we bought from Joe Rogers for fifty thousand dollars and asked him to read it and let me know what he thought of it. Twenty minutes later he put the manuscript on my desk and said, Forget it. I told him we'd paid fifty thousand dollars for that story. Even so, he said, forget it, the story's no good. It's dead. Yes, and it *is* dead.

HAMMER
He should have read the story before we bought it.

MANHEIM
We bought it two years ago. We've spent another fifty thousand on it, trying to fix it up. Finally, we went back to the story Rogers sold us, but it's no use, it's just naturally dead, that's all.

HAMMER
Who was it liked the story, when we bought it?

MANHEIM
Paul Cohan, and *he's* dead.

HAMMER
That son of a bitch. Where's Rogers? Let's get him here at a thousand a week, keep him for ten weeks—ten thousand dollars—make him write another story—get us even.

MANHEIM
    He's dead, too.

HAMMER
    I didn't know that. Wasn't Rogers a young man?

MANHEIM
    He was—thirty-nine. Heart attack.

HAMMER
    That son of a bitch—well, junk the God damn story and forget
    it. Just forget it. I'm getting old, that's all. Find out where that
    guttersnipe is and get him back here. He's around some place.
    In the Commissary, asking some waitress a lot of questions, or
    maybe in some star's dressing room, asking her all kinds of
    questions.

            (MANHEIM lifts the telephone receiver. HAMMER slaps his
            hand)

    Get away from that! I could do that myself. Go out and find
    him, talk to him, bring him back to his office.

MANHEIM
    I'm sorry, Patrick.
        (Pause)

HAMMER
    I'm sorry too, Ben.
        (He sighs)
    I'm old. Any time anybody does a thing like that to you, you
    ought to bust him in the mouth, the way you used to do when
    you were a kid.

MANHEIM
    It's all right, Patrick. I understand. And I'm not a kid any more.

HAMMER
        (After a pause)
    You do remember, then?
    18

MANHEIM

I remember.

HAMMER

It's a long, long time since we started out together in New York.
 (Rubbing his mouth with his left hand)
I thought you'd forgotten, Ben. I hadn't, but I thought you had.

MANHEIM

Well, Patrick, I hadn't *remembered*, either. I'll go see if I can find him.

HAMMER

Wait—wait a minute, Ben. I don't know what to tell him. Let me think a moment.
 (He thinks)
What people?

MANHEIM

What's that?

HAMMER

You said he has people with him all the time. What people?

MANHEIM

Well, they're all kinds—poets, clowns, gamblers, fortune-tellers, saints, eccentrics.

HAMMER

You *believe* all that?

MANHEIM

Yes, I do.

HAMMER

Are those people with *you*, too?

MANHEIM

Not many of them—any more. There used to be a *lot* of them

with me, but some *I* got rid of, and others just wandered away. They got tired of *me*. They're all with him, though.

HAMMER

You really think he's a great man, don't you?

MANHEIM

No, but he's *trying*. If you believe in people, you've got to believe in *anybody* who's trying. He can write. The best I can do is read.

HAMMER

Well, I can't write and I sure as hell *won't* read, but I've built up this great organization, so who the hell is *he*? They tell me pictures have had a greater influence on the human race than any other art—in practically no time at all, too. And I make *more* pictures than any other outfit in the world, and *better* ones. I'm not trusting you alone, Ben. I believe everything you say about him, but he's said the same things himself—in his own way, without saying *anything* at all most of the time, or talking about something else—about me getting my hands manicured. He got Rose the manicurist so excited, she couldn't finish her work. These three fingers aren't manicured. Go out and find him, talk to him, bring him back—get him to write Ave Maria for me.

MANHEIM

(*Amused*)
It's not as serious as all that, Patrick. You're just a little tired. Maybe you ought to take a rest. Go away for a month or two. Come back fresh.

(HAMMER *stands suddenly. He begins to reach very high,
as* HARRY *had done*)

What are you doing that for?

HAMMER

I don't *need* a rest.
(*He stands on the platform*)

20

MANHEIM
What's the matter?

HAMMER
I don't need a rest—understand?
(He jumps off the platform, lands heavily, looks at BEN)
Go get that son of a bitch.

(The curtain begins to come down)

He knows me, and I know him. I go around with a few people myself.

CURTAIN

ACT ONE Scene Two

An hour later.

HARRY BIRD *is seated at a small desk in his office, tap-ping at a typewriter. The pianola is going strong. Up the steps comes* SAM.

SAM *is a red-faced young man, probably Irish, who is always more than half-drunk, outwardly calm but in reality tense and nervous. He goes to the blackboard, erases the words,* Who is Sam, *stretches out on the divan. When the telephone rings* SAM *reaches over, lifts the receiver and very softly says,* "Yeah?" *He listens a mo-ment, then turns to* HARRY.

SAM

Shut it off, will you? I can't hear.

(HARRY *shuts off the pianola*)

Yeah—he's here.
(*Pause*)
Tell him to come right up.
(*He hangs up*)
It's the New York *Times* correspondent. He wants an interview.

HARRY

What did you tell him?

SAM

I told him to come right up.

HARRY

(*Turns on the pianola*)
Who told you to say that?

22

SAM

A little more publicity won't do you any harm. Especially in New York. Besides, I get lonely. I like to see people.

> (*The telephone rings again.* SAM *answers it, listens a moment*)

Who? Betty Fitch?

> (*Very calmly*)

It's a player-piano.

> (*Pause*)

I don't like it myself, Miss Fitch, but *he* likes it.

> (*Pause*)

Yes, I know who you are.

> (*He listens*)

Harry Bird—yes, ma'am. No, he's not an actor, he's a writer. My name is Sam—just Sam.

> (*Pause*)

I'll tell him.

> (*He turns to* HARRY)

Harry, Betty Fitch doesn't want you to play the piano any more. She's trying to study a part. She's a star, Harry—turn it off, will you?

HARRY

Hang up, Sam—just hang up.

> (SAM *hangs up, and stretches out.* HARRY *goes back to his typewriter. The telephone rings again.* SAM *reaches for it, but* HARRY *stops him. He lets the telephone ring three times, shuts off the piano, and then lifts the receiver*)

Madam Hammer's laundry. Good afternoon.

> (*He listens a moment, holds the receiver at arm's length while an excited female voice screams along. When there is silence,* HARRY *speaks*)

Excuse me, ma'am, could you repeat that? I didn't quite get it.

> (*He holds the telephone at arm's length and again the screaming is heard. When there is silence, he speaks again*)

23

I'm sorry, ma'am, but I just don't seem to be able to understand what it is you want. Now, if it's money you want, I'm afraid you're talking to the wrong man. This is Harry Bird. If you want romance, champagne, bright lights, and stuff like that, you're still talking to the wrong man. But—if it's immortality you want, you're talking to the *right* man.

> (*The New York Times* CORRESPONDENT *comes in and stands by*)

SAM

Ah, come on now, don't make her sore. What did she ever do to you?

HARRY

> (*With his hand over the mouthpiece*)

She married that phoney from Bulgaria a year ago, didn't she? What's his name?

SAM

You mean Polikey Vitrolin?

HARRY

Yeah—that's the guy. Comes to this country with his polite manners, and marries one of our sweetest high-school girls for six months.

> (*Into the telephone*)

Miss Fitch, you should never ought to have married that bad man from Bulgaria—a young innocent American girl from Cincinnati like you.

> (*He hangs up*)

CORRESPONDENT

Excuse me, Mr. Bird. I'm the correspondent of the New York Times.

> (*He extends his hand to* SAM)

SAM

Wait a minute—

24

HARRY

Mr. Bird is a little tired. Even so, I'm sure he'll be glad to answer your questions. But please don't ask him to get up.

CORRESPONDENT

(*To* SAM)

I can come back some other day, Mr. Bird, if you're not feeling well.

SAM

(*Taking a swallow from a bottle*)

I feel fine.

HARRY

Just draw up a chair, and make yourself at home.

(CORRESPONDENT *sits*)

Mr. Bird, would you like some pianola music perhaps?

SAM

No, Sam—if it's all the same to you, I'd like some *real* piano music.

HARRY

You shall have real piano music.

(*To the* CORRESPONDENT)

Mr. Bird sometimes prefers pianola music—for its pathos and comedy, for its humble American majesty—and then again he sometimes prefers straight piano music.

(*He dials a number*)

Music Department? This is Harry Bird's office. Mr. Bird would be deeply grateful if you would send your finest pianist to his office immediately, to play—a little Brahms, Mozart, Chopin. Yes—immediately, please. An old pianist or a young one—it doesn't matter, but don't send a dwarf or a Hindu—just somebody plain and skillful—no personality stuff. Yes—thank you.

(*He hangs up*)

Go ahead. Mr. Bird is ready for you.

CORRESPONDENT
    (To SAM)
Well, Mr. Bird, it wasn't easy to find your office, and I must say I didn't expect it to be quite so—well, shall we say, interesting?

SAM
Sure—let's say interesting.

CORRESPONDENT
What are all these things around here for—atmosphere?

SAM
This room used to be where the studio photographed its stars.

CORRESPONDENT
I see. Well, it's an unusual office for a writer, but I suppose it's what you want.

SAM
It's comfortable.

CORRESPONDENT
I see.
    (Pause)
Well, Mr. Bird, first, just what are your plans in the moving picture business?

SAM
    (Wearily, dead-pan)
I intend to revolutionize the industry.

CORRESPONDENT
I see. How do you intend to do it?

SAM
By thinking clearly. Right now I'm biding my time, but I *study* pictures every day.

26

CORRESPONDENT

I see. What sort of pictures do you study?

SAM

Old, silent pictures.

CORRESPONDENT

Why are you studying them?

SAM

Because I missed some of them when they came out.

CORRESPONDENT

(Making notes)
I see.
(Pause)
But the rumor around town is that you are going to write a story which has long been a favorite of Mr. Hammer's. Is that true?

SAM

(Stumped)
Ask Sam.

CORRESPONDENT

(Looking at HARRY)
And who is Sam, Mr. Bird? Your agent?

HARRY

No, I'm Mr. Bird's occasional drinking companion. We met at Tia Juana two years ago, and Mr. Bird was kind enough to remember me.

SAM

You were kind enough to remember me. I should find it very lonely here without a level-headed, comic, imaginative young man like you to keep me company now and then—not too often, though. Even brilliance can become tiresome. But tell the man about the rumor.

27

HARRY

Briefly, Mr. Bird feels that any favorite story of Mr. Hammer's will have to be written by Mr. Hammer himself.

CORRESPONDENT

I see. But only this morning *The Daily Reporter* ran a story to the effect that Mr. Bird, after three weeks of motion picture study, was now ready to go to work on an untitled story based on some themes and ideas of Mr. Hammer's.

HARRY

Mr. Hammer owns and operates *The Daily Reporter.*
     (*At the window*)
There goes Mark Spencer again!
     (*Shouting*)
Hi-ya, Mark!
     (*He turns*)
You'd think a big man like Mark Spencer would be humble enough to greet somebody unimportant, wouldn't you?

CORRESPONDENT

Have you met Mr. Spencer?

HARRY

No, I haven't met him in person, but I've seen him in a lot of pictures at neighborhood theaters. If I was famous and somebody I didn't know hollered out to me, Hi-ya, Sam, I think I'd holler back. Wouldn't you?

CORRESPONDENT

Yes, I believe I would, although I'm not sure. I'm not famous. Perhaps Mr. Bird can answer your question, Sam.

HARRY

How about it, Mr. Bird? Would you holler back?

SAM

If I was famous, I'd cut my throat.

28

CORRESPONDENT

But, Mr. Bird, you *are* famous.

SAM

Don't be silly. Interview Sam—he can answer your questions as well as I can.

CORRESPONDENT

Interview *Sam*, Mr. Bird?

SAM

Sure—sure. He's not a writer, but he's got an opinion or two about anything—the same as anybody else. Go ahead, ask him something. He'll give you a good answer.

CORRESPONDENT

(*Unsure*)

I see. Well, Sam, how long have you known Mr. Bird?

HARRY

As I said, the first time I met him was about two years ago at Tia Juana just after the fifth race. He'd won three hundred dollars on a long-shot named Blackrock, I believe, and he asked if I could use twenty dollars. I could, but I *wouldn't*. He then asked if I had a good horse in the next race, and I didn't. We've been friends ever since. When I say we've been friends I mean if he's down here we hang around together until I get bored or he gets bored. *I* get bored, too, you know.

CORRESPONDENT

I see. I'll put that down. Well, Sam, how does it feel to have a famous writer for a friend?

HARRY

(*Taking bottle from* SAM *for a swig*)

The same as having anybody else for a friend. Go ahead, Mr. Bird, take a sip.

29

SAM

Thank you, Sam.
(SAM *takes a swig*)

CORRESPONDENT

Well, Mr. Bird, how does it feel to have Sam for a friend?

SAM

I have never pushed the matter to the point of friendship.
A friend is taken to mean somebody who will do something for
you. I don't want anybody to do anything for me, and I know
Sam wouldn't *let* anybody do anything for him.

HARRY

(*At the window*)
Wait a minute—here comes somebody who *looks* like somebody. Come on, take a look at her.

(*The* CORRESPONDENT *goes to the window*)

Come on, Mr. Bird, take a look—it'll do you good.

(SAM *gets up and goes to the window*)

Who is that girl?

CORRESPONDENT

Nobody, most likely—looks like an extra.

HARRY

You mean a girl that beautiful is only an extra?

SAM

If she's that beautiful, she's an extra.

HARRY

Well, look at that, will you? Probably from Cincinnati.

SAM

They don't *all* come from Cincinnati.

HARRY

Most of them do.
>   (*Suddenly, loudly, leaning out of the window*)
Hey!—You!

GIRL'S VOICE

Who—me?

HARRY

Yes—you. You're from Cincinnati, aren't you?

GIRL'S VOICE

No, I'm from Montana. Great Falls.

HARRY

>   (*To the* PIANIST, *a small man, who has just come up the stairs*)
She's from Great Falls. (*Shouting, to the girl*) What's your name?

GIRL'S VOICE

Martha Harper.

HARRY

>   (*To* PIANIST)
Martha Harper—you never know who they are till you ask them.
>   (*Out the window, to the girl*)
Well, Martha, good luck. You're going to be great.
>   (*He waves*)

GIRL'S VOICE

Are you a producer? I want to meet a producer.

>   (HARRY *points to the piano. The* PIANIST *goes to the piano, sits down, adjusts some music before him, and begins to play Brahms: the "Double Concerto." The telephone rings.* SAM *goes over and answers it.* HARRY *leans out the window*)

31

SAM

> (On telephone)

Yeah.

> (He listens)

I'm sorry, Miss Fitch—but what you are now hearing is Brahms. It is positively not a machine. There is a small man here seated at the piano, and it's *him*.

> (He hangs up)

GIRL'S VOICE

I want to know a producer. I'd like him to be a young producer, but if I can't meet a young one, I guess I'll just have to be satisfied with an old one.

HARRY

Come on up, will you? For the love of God, come on up.

CORRESPONDENT

> (To SAM)

But, Mr. Bird, don't you think Sam ought to be a little more—

SAM

No, no—Sam's all right.

HARRY

> (Looking down the stairs)

Here she comes. Look at her.

> (With delight)

There you are. Come right up now. One step at a time. Up you go! Come on, Martha Harper.

> (The girl comes up the stairs. HARRY stands back, admiring her. She's in a classic costume, and very pretty. HARRY puts his arms around her and kisses her)

MARTHA

You are a producer! What's your name?

HARRY

My name is Harry Bird.

(The CORRESPONDENT *looks from* HARRY *to* SAM, *confused*)

I don't generally tell my name to young girls from Great Falls, Montana, who want to be in pictures—but I'm afraid I must tell you.

(*Very seriously suddenly*)

Don't you know any better than to go around looking for producers?

MARTHA

Oh, I'm ready for them. If that's the way to get in pictures, I'm going to do it. I've made up my mind.

HARRY

(*Swiftly*)

The interview is over. Sam! Herr Brahms!

(*The man at the piano stops playing*)

If you don't mind, I'd like to have a few minutes with Miss Harper alone.

(*He points to the steps going down*)

MARTHA

But I like music. Can't he go on playing?

(SAM *takes the* CORRESPONDENT *by the arm to the head of the stairway. They are met by* MISS FITCH *coming up*)

BETTY

Oh, there you are—you, you—!

SAM

He's not Harry Bird. This is the correspondent of the New York *Times*.

BETTY

Oh, so you're Mr. Bird?

33

SAM

Now, wait a minute.

BETTY

Well, listen to me, Mr. Bird, you've got to stop that God damn piano, do you hear?

SAM

This is my office, and Mr. Hammer himself told me to listen to the piano as much as I like—to inspire me.

BETTY

Inspire you? What about *me*? Inspire you to do *what*?

SAM

To write philosophical things.

BETTY

Philosophical?

SAM

That's right. Have you ever stopped to think, Miss Fitch, how wonderful the human body is just from the point of view of plumbing?

BETTY

Plumbing? What are you trying to do, kid me?

SAM

I wouldn't think of it. Mr. Hammer wants me to get inspired and write him a great story. I'm doing my best. A piano helps me.

BETTY

Well, it doesn't help *me*—all day long. All—day—long. I'm going crazy.

MARTHA

Excuse me, Miss Fitch, could I have your autograph?

34

BETTY
>(Graciously, but phoney)
Of course. May I have a pen, please?

SAM
Won't a pencil do?

>(The CORRESPONDENT hands her a fountain pen)

BETTY
>(Angry and impatient, to SAM and the CORRESPONDENT)
All right, give me a piece of paper to autograph on, will you?
What are you waiting for?

MARTHA
Excuse me, Miss Fitch. Could you autograph on me instead of
on a piece of paper?

BETTY
On you?

MARTHA
>(Lowering her waist)
Yes. Right here. Over my heart. I'll put some scotch tape over
it when I take a bath so it won't come off. Please, Miss Fitch,
I've worshiped you from afar.

BETTY
Well—all right.
>(She begins to write her name on MARTHA, but the pen
is bad and she has to shake it several times)

HARRY
Easy there, Miss Fitch, if you please. Don't hurt her. She's
flesh and blood just like anybody else.

BETTY
I'm not hurting her.
>(Writing)

35

Autographs, autographs—you'd think people would have a little consideration for the thoughts and moods of others.

SAM

Thoughts and moods?

BETTY

(*Shouting*)
Yes, thoughts and moods!

SAM

Oh.

HARRY

(*To* MARTHA, *who is showing him* BETTY FITCH's *autograph*)
It's very pretty, Martha.

(*The* PIANIST *is eager to see*)

Here, show it to him, too.

(*The* PIANIST *looks*)

Pretty, isn't it?

PIANIST

Prettiest I ever saw.
(*He goes right on playing*)

MARTHA

I'll never wash it off.

BETTY

(*To* SAM)
For one moment at least, will you be good enough to ask that man at the piano to stop?

SAM

But, Miss Fitch, I'm trying to become inspired, so I can think philosophical thoughts. What kind of thoughts do you think?

36

BETTY
> (*Seriously*)
> I think philosophical thoughts, too.

SAM
> You do?

BETTY
> Like, Who am I? Why did it have to be me? Where did I come from?

SAM
> You're from Cincinnati, aren't you?

BETTY
> (*With contempt*)
> Cincinnati?
> (*Proudly*)
> I'm from New York.

SAM
> Then you *do* know where you're from.

BETTY
> I don't mean like that, from cities. I mean, from what have I come, to what am I going? You know what I mean, don't you?

SAM
> Yes, I sure do. A man like me who's paid a lot of money to get inspired and write philosophical things has got to understand a girl like you, Miss Fitch, or get out of the business.
>
> (BEN MANHEIM *comes up the stairs. He stands a moment, looking around*)

BETTY
> (*Bitterly, swiftly*)
> I've got to talk to you, Mr. Manheim, about this lousy part they're trying to push down my throat in *Danger Street.*

37

MANHEIM
    (Gently)
Some other time, please.

BETTY
    (Furious, almost screaming)
Well, I don't like the part, see? And I won't do it, that's all.
I'll break my contract.

SAM
    (Taking her by the arm, and going down the steps)
Ah, what do you want to get sore at the man for? What difference does it make what part you get? You're a great actress.

CORRESPONDENT
    (Following them)
But, Mr. Bird, what about our interview? What am I going to
tell the New York *Times?*

MANHEIM
Harry, if you don't mind, I'd like to have a little of your time—
alone.

HARRY
I don't mind. We're aione enough.
    (Of the PIANIST*)*
Let him play.
    (To the PIANIST*)*
Play a lot of things. She likes it. What else have you brought
along?

PIANIST
I've got some Chopin.

HARRY
Play some of that.
    (To MANHEIM*)*

Sit down. This girl's from Great Falls, Montana. She's looking for a young producer. Her name's Martha Harper.

MANHEIM
How do you do?

MARTHA
(*Moving toward* MANHEIM)
Are you a producer?

HARRY
Here, Martha. Stretch out on this divan, and listen to the music.

(MARTHA *stretches out.* HARRY *stands back and admires her, while* BEN MANHEIM *watches*)

She just had Miss Fitch autograph her body. Want to see it?

MANHEIM
No, I don't believe I do.

HARRY
It's very pretty.

MARTHA
Is it really pretty?
(*She pushes down her shirt. The* PIANIST *turns to watch*)
It's upside down for me.
(*She spells the name*)
B-e-t-t-y, Betty. F-i-t-c-h, Fitch. Betty Fitch!

HARRY
(*Over to one side, while* MARTHA *listens to the music*)
Oh, thou most beautiful among women—

MANHEIM
(*Softly*)
You shouldn't be cruel, Harry.

HARRY

I'm *not* being cruel.

MANHEIM

It's not easy to believe you'd make fun of an unfortunate girl.

HARRY

I'm *not* making fun of her. I don't think you understand.

MANHEIM

If there's anything to understand, I'm afraid I don't.

HARRY

Well, briefly, there's the story.

MANHEIM

Ave Maria?

HARRY

Yes.

MANHEIM

But who is she?

HARRY

She's nobody. She's a kid from Great Falls, Montana. I met her five minutes ago. She was walking down the company street. I'm going to write the story—but only for her.

MANHEIM

But Mr. Hammer wants Margaret Corrigan for the girl.

HARRY

Margaret Corrigan? Who's she?

MANHEIM

One of our actresses. Mr. Hammer wants to introduce her to the public in Ave Maria.

HARRY
> (*Shaking his head*)
No—nothing doing—

MANHEIM
You mean you'll write the story if this girl gets the part?

HARRY
That's *exactly* what I mean.

MANHEIM
Have you got a story?

HARRY
I have.
> (*He looks at the girl*)
—Now.

MANHEIM
> (*Looking at the girl, then at* HARRY)
Harry, you're not—?

HARRY
No, no—don't offend me. I don't want anything from her. But
there she is—for everybody. She's no whore yet, but she's about
to become one. You can be sure it won't be from anything but
beautiful, idiotic innocence and love, though.

MANHEIM
But Mr. Hammer expects the story to be inspirational—religious, even.

HARRY
The story *is* going to be inspirational, as you say—and religious,
too. Not because Mr. Hammer expects it to be, but because
there's no other way to look at anything. What could you do
but love her? Could you mock her? Make little of her spirit's
littleness? Laugh at her fool's blessed heart?

41

MANHEIM

Are you sure, Harry, you're not having fun—from being bored?

HARRY

I am having fun, but not from being bored. For the first time since I've been out here, I'm delighted. I've found a woman who's innocent.

MANHEIM

I can't believe you're not serious, and I can't believe you are.

HARRY

I am serious.

MANHEIM

But this poor girl. Let's be honest. She's ordinary. She's a common, everyday—
(Pause)

HARRY

You needn't hesitate, Ben. She's a woman. If we call her names, it's still herself we mean.

MANHEIM

There's a million girls like this girl, Harry.

HARRY

There's more than a million like her. There's none unlike her, and she is like the others most. She is their best beauty, their awfulest inconsequence, their most gathered glory.

MANHEIM

Aren't you giving her just a little too much importance?

HARRY

I am not, even though it is the function of art to give all things more importance than it would seem they deserve at first. She cannot be given too much importance. She is the mother of everybody.

42

PIANIST

What'll I play now?

HARRY

Try "Ave Maria."

PIANIST

Schubert or Gounod?

HARRY

Schubert first, then Gounod.

PIANIST

O.K.

(*He begins to play Schubert's "Ave Maria"*)

HARRY

(*Slowly, moving toward* MARTHA)
Hail Mary. Full of grace. The Lord is with thee. Blessed art thou, and blessed is the fruit of thy womb. Pray for us sinners now and at the hour of our death. Amen.

MARTHA

What did you say?

HARRY

I said, How do you like it out here in California?

MARTHA

Oh, I like it fine.

HARRY

How old are you, Martha?

MARTHA

Nineteen.

HARRY

When did you first go with a man? Do you understand?

43

MARTHA

Oh, I understand all right.

MANHEIM

(*Objecting sincerely*)
Harry, you've got no right—

HARRY

(*Stopping him*)
Wait a minute, Ben.

MARTHA

If I tell you, will you give me a job in pictures?

HARRY

Yes, I promise.

MARTHA

Will I be a star?

HARRY

Yes, you will.

MARTHA

You're not fooling me, are you? I thought producers wanted more than *answers* to *questions*. But I don't care *what* they want. I'll give it to them, just so I can be a star.

HARRY

I'm not fooling you.

MARTHA

I guess I was almost eleven.

MANHEIM

(Angry)
Harry, I think this has gone far enough.

44

HARRY
  (*Swiftly, turning*)
I'm sorry, Ben. But you don't understand.

MARTHA
What's the matter?

HARRY
Martha, I ask you humbly to forgive me.

MARTHA
Oh, it's all right. It was so long ago. But I didn't know anything, then.

MANHEIM
  (*Bitterly*)
You're lying! You're lying!

MARTHA
  (*To* HARRY)
I'm not lying. I was eleven. Will you put me in pictures?

MANHEIM
  (*Deeply hurt*)
I don't believe you. I don't believe a word you've said. You're
a mischievous, ambitious young girl.
  (*He brings all the currency out of his wallet*)
I want you to go home. Here's money. Take it and go home.

MARTHA
You mean to my room at the Studio Club?

MANHEIM
I mean to Great Falls, Montana. Here, take the money.

MARTHA
I have no home in Great Falls.

45

MANHEIM

> (*Almost irritated*)

Well, go somewhere. Don't stay here.

MARTHA

But I want to be in pictures.

MANHEIM

> (*Turning to* HARRY)

You're not going to be taken in by this girl's incredible performance, are you? Look at her. Anybody can see no man in the world has touched her—yet. And it would make me most unhappy if anyone I knew touched her.

MARTHA

What's the matter with me? I went to a doctor last week—

HARRY

> (*Swiftly*)

Did he make love to you?

MANHEIM

> (*Almost insane with rage*)

You've got to stop asking these ugly and unkind questions. I won't allow it. You know very well the girl is not telling the truth. I'm not a young man and it's a long time since I raised a hand against another, but if you ask this girl another question I swear—

HARRY

Take it easy, Ben. I know. You've got a daughter of your own about her age.

> (MANHEIM *takes a swipe at* HARRY. HARRY *moves with it, so that he is not touched.* MANHEIM *loses his balance and falls.* HARRY *helps him up.* MANHEIM *is terribly shaken and embarrassed*)

46

MARTHA

    What's the matter?

HARRY

    I'm sorry, Ben.

MANHEIM

        (*Almost unable to speak*)
    It's all right. I think I'd better go now.

HARRY

    No—wait.
        (*Pause, earnestly*)
    I want to write the story.
        (*Pause*)
    Even so, I'll not tell Mr. Hammer.

MANHEIM

    I understand. Thanks very much.
        (*Pause*)
    I'll tell him. Will you be here awhile? Mr. Hammer may want
to have another talk with you.

HARRY

    I'll wait till I hear from you.

        (MANHEIM *goes. There is a long pause, during which*
        HARRY *looks at* MARTHA, *almost embarrassed, and she*
        at him)

MARTHA

        (*With effort*)
    Who was that man?

HARRY

        (*His voice hushed*)
    Ben Manheim. He's the First Assistant to Mr. Hammer.

MARTHA

Who's *he?*

HARRY

He's the man who started this institution.

MARTHA

Oh.
(*Pause*)
Am I *really* going to be in pictures?

HARRY

Yes, you are.

MARTHA

Then, I sure would like to meet a famous actor.

HARRY

(*He walks around, troubled. He looks at her strangely.
He speaks swiftly and terribly*)
Now! Why did you lie to me?

MARTHA

(*Swiftly, defensively*)
I didn't lie.

HARRY

(*Touching the* PIANIST's *shoulder*)
O.K., that's all. Thanks a lot.
(*He waits for the* PIANIST *to go*)
You can stop acting now. Why did you lie?

MARTHA

(*Embarrassed*)
I don't know.

HARRY

Why did you ask Miss Fitch to autograph you, instead of a
piece of paper?

48

MARTHA

Because I knew she'd do it, out of ridiculous and pathetic pride. Because she's been made inhuman and vulgar by her cheap fame.

HARRY

Why did you pretend to be stupid?

MARTHA

You *wanted* me to be stupid, shouting at me from a window. But even if I *were* stupid, you had no right to be, too. I *had to* be stupid because . . .
>   (*Pause*)

HARRY

Yes?

MARTHA

Because I was so eager for you to know me.
>   (*Pause*)
I know from your writing that you *ought* to know me.

HARRY

You know my writing?

MARTHA

Yes, I do. You're not a bad writer. You oughtn't to be cruel.

HARRY

I'm not *always* cruel.

MARTHA

You were cruel to *me*. I suppose almost everybody you meet is cruel, but that's no excuse for you. You're still young enough to have fun, but you're never so young you can have the kind of fun that hurts others.
>   (*Pause*)
You ought to be ashamed.

49

HARRY

    (Quietly, seriously)
I am. Is there anything I can do?

MARTHA

Nothing. Now.
    (She prepares to go)
But I *am* sorry about Mr. Manheim.

HARRY

Then why didn't you tell *him* the truth?

MARTHA

How could I? He was right, but he didn't really *believe* he was
right. If I told him the truth, he would despise *me* even more
than *her*.

HARRY

Her? Who?

MARTHA

The Woman. Oh, I could be *her*. I could play *that* part.
    (Pause)
It's a pity I'm not going to.

HARRY

Why not?

MARTHA

I'm not going to play the part because I don't think you can
write it. I'm sorry if you're hurt. Good-by.
    (She begins to go)

HARRY

    (Almost shouting)
Hurt? What the hell are you talking about? Nothing can hurt
me. Wait a minute—what do you mean I can't write it?

50

(He stands at the head of the steps)

I can write anything, and better than anybody else in the world.

(The downstairs door closes. HARRY *hurries to the window)*

Now, listen, you—I admit I was a fool. But that's finished.

(He begins to shout)

I'm warning you, I'm not going to try to find you. But I'm asking you to come back—

(Pause)

O.K. So long.

(Softly)

And go to hell.

(He turns away from the window, troubled and amazed. He starts the pianola. The telephone rings, but he refuses to answer it. At last he sits down wearily, and after a moment buries his face in his hands. HAMMER *and* MANHEIM *come into the room. He doesn't look up until* HAMMER *speaks)*

HAMMER

My boy—my boy! Ben's told me the good news. Let me shake your hand.

HARRY

O.K., shake it.

(He thrusts out his hand, but does not get up. HAMMER *refuses to take his hand)*

HAMMER

What's the matter?

(He shuts off the pianola)

Now, what's the matter, Harry? You can tell me.

HARRY

(Wearily)

I want to write the story—

HAMMER

Yes—Ben told me—and I'm going to see that you have everything you want. Everything—

HARRY

(*Stands*)
Thanks—I *want* to write the story, but I know I can't.

HAMMER

Why not?

HARRY

(*Angry*)
I just don't understand things well enough. I need more time. Later, maybe.

HAMMER

You mean a week?

HARRY

I mean five years—maybe *ten*.
(*He begins to throw darts idly, while* HAMMER *and* MANHEIM *watch*)

HAMMER

(*Whispering*)
In ten years I'll be seventy-three years old.
(HAMMER *throws a dart. Then* MANHEIM *throws one.* MARTHA *comes in.* HARRY *turns, sees her, and without a word goes to her. He stands about three paces from her, looking at her, amazed and delighted.* MANHEIM *turns and watches, too.* MANHEIM *and* HAMMER *look at one another.* MARTHA *moves to* HARRY. *She stands very close to him, then leans forward and very slowly kisses him.* HARRY *puts his arms around her, and the curtain begins to come down*)
Is that one of our stars, or an extra? Who is that girl?

CURTAIN

The time is once again a moment or two before the curtain fell. As it rises, HAMMER *says:*

HAMMER
Is that one of our stars, or an extra? Who is that girl?

(HARRY *and* MARTHA *stand apart, looking at one another.* HAMMER *goes over to them*)

Let me give you some advice, young woman. If you think the way to get into pictures is to throw yourself at a writer or a producer, you're sadly mistaken. That procedure went out with silent pictures. Making moving pictures is not only a big business, it is an important art, with tremendous responsibilities. Responsibilities to the country at large, and to all of its people, without regard for race, color or creed. Responsibilities to men, women, and children—and, yes—to *generations* still unborn. The very first need of this industry is stories, and where do stories come from? They come from writers.

(*The curtain begins to come down*)

What do you mean coming in here and kissing this writer? What do you mean stopping this man when he is about to go to work?

(*The curtain is down. Almost instantly it rises again.* MARTHA *is standing alone on the platform,* HAMMER *has one foot on the first step of the platform, and is talking to her.* BEN MANHEIM *is watching, a little confused.* HARRY BIRD *is walking to* MARTHA. HAMMER *continues*)

53

I know what a temptation it is for a pretty girl to sell her body for a chance at fame and fortune, but there are other writers.

> (*The curtain begins to fall again.* HARRY BIRD *is on the platform, beside* MARTHA)

HARRY

> (*Almost comically*)

Ah, shut up.

> (*The curtain is down. Almost instantly it rises again, and now* BEN MANHEIM *is talking to* HAMMER, *as if he were trying to keep a good fellow out of a street brawl*)

MANHEIM

You're wasting your breath, Patrick. Come on, let's go back to your office.

HAMMER

Go back to my office? Why? Who is this girl?

> (*He tries to push around* MANHEIM *to see* MARTHA. *He shouts*)

Who are you?

MARTHA

My name is Martha Harper. I want to be in pictures. I don't care how I get in, or what I have to do. All I want is fame and money. I want people to point at me as I pass by. I want little children to run after my automobile. I don't care what I have to do. I'll do it.

> (*To* HARRY, *softly*)

Do you want to know me?

HARRY

I do know you, and I want you to know me. Go change your clothes and come right back. We're going on a trip.

> (*She goes. The curtain begins to come down*)

54

HAMMER

    (*To* MANHEIM, *as if he were deaf*)
What did she say? Now, Ben, get the hell out of my way and
let me talk to Harry.

    (MANHEIM *and* HAMMER *begin to struggle. The curtain is
    down. It rises almost instantly.* MANHEIM *and* HAMMER
    are clutching at one another. HARRY BIRD *is printing the
    last two letters of "Ave Maria" on the blackboard, and*
    SAM *comes in with his hand over his left eye*)

SAM

    (*To* HARRY)
That ridiculous actress Betty Fitch hit me in the eye.
    (*He goes to the water jar, moistens his handkerchief and
    puts it over his eye*)

HARRY

Whoever told you cold water is good for a black eye?

SAM

Nobody, but I haven't got anything else to put on it. What are
these boys wrestling about?

HARRY

About the future of the American moving picture.

SAM

    (*With bottle*)
I never saw a woman with so many phoney ideas.
    (SAM *takes a swig*)
She says she's going to have me arrested.

    (MANHEIM *and* HAMMER *stop wrestling*)

HARRY

What do you mean? You didn't try anything funny on her,
did you?

SAM

It wasn't funny. I can't resist a phoney woman. They do something to me. I sat around for ten minutes talking about philosophical moods and thoughts, and that's as long as I could take it. There's nothing in her dressing room but a wonderful pink couch. What else could I do? What would you do?

HAMMER

Excuse me, young man. I don't know who you are, or what you've been up to, but if you're a friend of Mr. Bird's, I'll protect you. Harry's going to write a great story for me and I don't want anything to interfere with his work. Who is it you've attacked?

SAM

You excuse me. I don't know who you are, or what you've been up to. I made a pass at that ridiculous woman, because I thought she was troubled and lonely, and expected me to.
      (To HARRY)
Who is this—whippersnapper?

HARRY

What do you mean who is he? He's one of the boys. He's got a stable of horses. You've bet on the Ave horses, haven't you? Ave Patrick. That's him. Ave Miss Henderson. That's his old secretary. Ave Ogelthorpe. That's the young producer who committed suicide last year—you know, the genius.

SAM

Is this Patrick Hammer?

HARRY

Sure. That's what I've been trying to tell you. Ave Dublin. That's where he was born. Ave New York. I don't know what that stands for.

SAM

I know the horses. Ave Money. There's one of the fastest

56

three-year-olds in the country, Mr. Hammer. I've followed your horses a good long time, and I've made money on them, too. I caught Ave Mother when she paid twenty to one at Pimlico. It was the Saturday before Mother's Day. It was just a hunch bet—ten across—but I got a potful of money. That race wasn't framed, was it?

HAMMER

Thoroughbred horses are only a hobby with me. I have nothing to do with their training or running.

SAM

How come? I thought you supervised everything. I thought you did a *lot* of betting.

HAMMER

I sometimes make a small wager on one of my horses.

SAM

Did you have anything on Ave Mother that time she paid twenty to one?

HAMMER

I don't see how it's any business of yours, but since you're a friend of Mr. Bird's—yes, I did.

SAM

How much?

HAMMER

A thousand dollars.

SAM

Track odds?

HAMMER

Yes, track odds.

57

SAM

Man, that's a lot of money—twenty thousand dollars for one thousand. You sure can pick them.

HAMMER

I'm partial to my own horses, and especially partial to the ones that seem to be coming into their best form.

SAM

Sure—sure. But that lousy Ave Truth was a no-good if I ever heard of one. Did he ever win a race?

HAMMER

Yes, he did—once.

SAM

How much did *he* pay?

HAMMER

About thirty to one.

SAM

What ever happened to him?

HAMMER

I sold him for nine thousand dollars. Three weeks later he broke a leg and was destroyed.

SAM

By God, it takes a smart man to know how to make money at a hobby, doesn't it?

(*The curtain begins to come down*)

HAMMER

Horse races are pure luck. I've been a lucky man all my life.

(*The curtain is down. It rises almost immediately.* HAMMER *is trying to talk to* HARRY, *who has just started the pianola*)

Now, Harry, about this girl—I know how it is with a young man, and I say God bless you and more power to you—but this is no time to let anything interfere with your work. Beautiful girls are a dime a dozen. I'll get you all you want. But first write the story. O.K.?

HARRY

I'm driving home to San Francisco tonight.
    (Pause)
It'll take me about two weeks to write the story.

HAMMER

That's a good boy. I can truthfully say I love you, Harry. I'll have Murphy draw up the contract immediately. How much advance do you want?

HARRY

I don't want *any* advance.

HAMMER

No advance? What do you mean? Take ten thousand anyway—for expenses.

HARRY

My expenses at home are about a dollar a day. At that rate, I've got enough for three years.

HAMMER

But we've got to have a contract, Harry.

HARRY

Why?

HAMMER

We always have a contract. We don't ask writers to write for nothing. We pay them, and we pay them well.

HARRY

I don't need any money to write.

59

HAMMER

Take the money, Harry. Listen to me. Take it. I'll get Murphy to draw up a contract immediately.

HARRY

No, thanks. I'll just go home and write the story. If it's good—if I like it—I'll send it down. Then if you like it, I'll talk to you about it.

HAMMER

Talk about *what*, Harry?

HARRY

About how much I'm willing to let you have it for—about who is to produce and direct it—about who is to appear in it.

HAMMER

Now, Harry, let me get Murphy to draw up a contract right here and now, while we're all enthusiastic.

HARRY

I'm not enthusiastic. I just want to go home and write the story.

HAMMER

Harry, don't think I'm not grateful to you for your honesty. You haven't allowed us to pay you one cent for the three weeks that you've been here. Time is money, and a writer's time is a *lot* of money. I know you wouldn't let yourself take something for nothing, and I appreciate and respect the way you feel. But now, Harry—now that you're going to go to work and write the story—let me hand you a check for ten thousand dollars—fifteen—twenty—or twenty-five, even. I'm an old gambler, and I know when I've got a sure thing. I'll bet my life you write a great story.

HARRY

I'm an old gambler myself. You'll be seeing me in two or three weeks.

(*He moves to go*)

60

HAMMER

Now, wait a minute, Harry. Let's get this thing straight.

HARRY

It's straight now. I'm not going to write the story for you. I'm going to write it for myself. You don't have to risk a penny of your money. I promise to offer you the story first, but you won't *have* to take it—

HAMMER

You're being unfair, Harry. The story is my idea. Even my horses are named Ave.

HARRY

Yeah. Ave Money.

HAMMER

Look at any scratch sheet. What kind of names do you read? Crazy. Why shouldn't the names of my horses be crazy, too? You can't go off this way, with nothing settled. I'm part of Ave Maria.

HARRY

You write your story. I'm going home to write mine.

HAMMER

(Severe and bitter)

Just a minute, young man. If you're not going to be nice—if you're trying to hurt me—don't forget that I can be as dirty as you can. *Dirtier*. For three long weeks I've tried to get along with you. I've humored you. I've let you have your way. I've given you this office and privileges I don't give anybody else. I've had old silent pictures flown out from New York for you in special airplanes. I've searched all over the country for a baby grand pianola. What for? I don't know. But now, if you're not going to be nice, I'll give you a performance you won't forget as long as you live. I come from the streets, too. Don't think I'm no match for you.

(Pause)

I don't *like* talking to you this way, Harry, because I know you're a genius, but you could be the world's greatest genius, and I still wouldn't give a good God damn if you tried to pull a fast one on me.

(*Gently*)

Let bygones be bygones, no hard feelings, and I'll telephone Murphy to come right over with a contract. It'll take only a few minutes.

(*He moves toward* HARRY *with his hand extended. He is smiling.* HARRY *takes his hand*)

My boy, I'm glad you're going to be with us. Let me be the first to welcome you.

(HARRY *releases* HAMMER's *hand*)

HARRY

Get away, old man! Get away!

HAMMER

(*Infuriated*)

Now, listen, you guttersnipe. Listen to me, before you go.

HARRY

(*Singing*)

For an old man he is old
And an old man he is gray

(MARTHA, *in her street clothes, comes in.* HARRY *embraces her, and speaks the following lines*)

But a young man's heart is full of love
Get away, old man, get away.

We're going to Mexico, Martha. We'll get married in Tia Juana. See you around, Sam. So long, Ben.

(*He goes with* MARTHA)

HAMMER

Stop him! Ben, stop him, will you? Go after him! He likes you!

Don't let him get away! Go get him. This is no time to go to Mexico. Ben, what are you standing there for?

MANHEIM
> (Seriously, troubled)
It's no use, Patrick. Let him go. I've been wrong about him all the time. He's no good. Forget the whole thing.

HAMMER
No, Ben. I'll go get him *myself*.
> (He begins to go. He stops at the steps, turns suddenly to SAM)
I don't know who you are, but if you can get him to go home and write the story, I'll give you anything you want. Anything.

SAM
What will you give me?

HAMMER
I'll give you a long-shot at Narragansett tomorrow. He'll be at least twenty to one.

SAM
Twenty to one isn't enough, because I've only got fourteen dollars to bet.

HAMMER
I'll give you the long-shot, and a hundred dollars.

SAM
O.K. What's the horse?

HAMMER
Get him to go home and start writing the story and I'll give you the horse.

SAM
I don't trust you.

HAMMER

All right. The horse is Ave Mother again. She hasn't been in the money in seven starts. She's going to win tomorrow. Now, go get him.

(*He hands* SAM *a hundred-dollar bill*)

SAM

(*Going*)

I don't know why you should trust me. I didn't trust you. Go get him yourself. He's my friend and I never interfere in the personal affairs of my friends.

(*He throws the money at* HAMMER, *and goes*)

HAMMER

(*Screaming*)

I lied to you! Ave Mother *isn't* going to win. I lied, I lied!

SAM

(*Going*)

I'll take a chance.

HAMMER

(*Almost pathetically*)

Well, Ben, they've beat me. I'm beat. I've got to sit down now. If the world wasn't in such a mess I'd drop everything and go back to Dublin and die. That's where I want to be. That's where I started and that's where I want to end. I tried my best. All my life I tried my best. But it's no use. I can't get good things out of myself, and I can't get them out of others. Get away, he told me. Get away, old man. Think of it! Get away— to me. I'm tired now. I'm beat.

(*Pause*)

Ben, what do you remember about your earliest years?

MANHEIM

(*Pause, slowly*)

I remember not getting enough to eat. I remember getting

64

pushed around, and then turning and pushing *others* around. Because they pushed *me*.

> (*Pause*)

Why?

HAMMER

Oh, nothing.

> (*Quietly*)

I remember things like that, too, Ben, but I remember other things, too. I remember a girl in Dublin. There was never born into this filthy world anyone more beautiful, more like an angel. I worshiped her. I kissed the door of her house late at night, getting up from bed to run there. One day I came face to face with her in the street. I was eight or nine, I guess, and so was she. I was so surprised to see her, so surprised to be seen by *her*, I stopped walking. I couldn't move. I couldn't breathe. All I could do was stare at her coming down the street toward me. I wanted to say something, but I couldn't think of anything to say. I don't know why I did it, but I began to whisper to her, "Ave Maria, full of grace, the Lord is with thee." She stopped and looked at me, and I believed she saw me—really saw *me*. I believed she *loved* me. I wanted nothing more of the world, nothing more of life, than to worship her, with all the innocence of a boy's heart. That's all I wanted, Ben. That's all I've ever wanted.

> (*Pause*)

Then she spit at me!

> (*He buries his head in his hands, and after a moment lifts it*)

I ran home. I went to my room and locked the door.

> (*Pause, quietly with anguish*)

I didn't leave the house for a month. I didn't want to go anywhere. I was afraid of the world. I was afraid of its people. My family couldn't understand. I couldn't tell them. They brought doctors and priests to talk to me, to pray for me. They thought I was going to die.

> (*Pause*)

65

My poor mother's secret tears—my poor father's silent grief—
These are things I can never forgive the world. A month is a
long time—a month of sorrow is a long, long time for a
boy. They were not wrong in fearing *that* I would die. I *did*
die, Ben. I was murdered! Murdered as if they had put a knife
in my heart. It would have been better for me to die in my
body as well as in my heart, but I would *not* die. In my body
I would stay among them—to pay them back for the tears of
my mother. Slowly, quietly, steadily—for the grief of my father.
"I'll pay them back. I'll stay alive to pay them back." And I
have paid them back. Their loveliest came to me as though I
were a Prince. They came not for the good in myself—not to
restore what they had murdered. They came humiliated, seeking my favor. In my heart I spit at *them*—for the shame of their
purposes—their women hating me and pretending in their
nakedness to love me. *They* are the ugly, Ben, not I. I have
never been fooled by them. I took their mothers before they
bore children or went to the marriage bed.

MANHEIM

 (*Sincerely*)
Patrick—these are not things to say.

HAMMER

They are, Ben—they are. I must tell you. I've told no one else.
I must tell you, and you must hear me out. I'm sick in my
heart, and old. All the ugly, lonely years have gone by. I have
made the far turn. I run wounded, as I started. I run bleeding,
in darkness, with all my might. I run as if I were going home,
Ben, but I have no home. Home is a street at night, a dark door
of a great house in which she slept. Home is where I was
murdered, where the love died in me, where the hate was born.
 (*Fiercely*)
I know he can write this story for me, Ben.

MANHEIM

He could never write a story like that.

66

HAMMER

(*Almost angry*)

Of course he can! Ben, we've known each other a long time. I went one way and you went another. I know the way I went, and you know the way you went. Maybe my way was not as right as yours, but if you love me, or even if you only pity me—in memory of all the years we've known one another—go to him, talk to him, be gentle, be generous in your heart— *I can't*—get him to go home and write the story. Before I die, I want to see it in pictures. Then I can go home—yes, Ben, I am going—but instead of being dead there, I'll be alive. Instead of hating, I'll love.

(*Pause.* MANHEIM *looks at* HAMMER *curiously. At last he puts his hand on* HAMMER'S *shoulder*)

MANHEIM

I'll go, Patrick.

(MANHEIM *goes. When the door is heard to shut at the foot of the steps,* HAMMER *leaps to his feet, almost in a fury. He walks around, back and forth, like a wild animal. He goes to the window and looks out. Then he goes to the pianola and starts it, listens a moment, then turns it off. He then goes to the telephone, and dials*)

HAMMER

(*On the telephone, in his genuine voice, strong and commanding*)

Mr. Hammer speaking. Let me speak to Miss Fitch, please.

(*Pause, irritated, almost shouting*)

I told you this is Mr. Hammer speaking. I don't care if she is in the shower. Just hand her the phone or get her out.

(*Pause*)

Betty?—Mr. Hammer.

(*He holds the telephone out at arm's length just as* HARRY *had done until the screaming ends*)

I know you're unhappy about the part in *Danger Street*. Why shouldn't you be unhappy? It's a lousy part. But what makes you think you deserve a better part?

67

(He holds the telephone at arm's length again)

Yes, yes, I know. Now, calm down. I'm thinking of putting another writer on the story. Yes. Yes. Now, send your maid away and I'll come down for a talk.

(Pause, while he holds the telephone out just a short distance from his ear. The woman's voice is warm and friendly now. He listens with an expression of terrible contempt, maybe for her, maybe for himself)

I'm not so happy myself, Betty. We'll sit down together, have a couple of drinks, and talk things over.

(Pause)

Five minutes? Nonsense. You don't need to dress for me. Just send the maid away.

(Pause)

That's a good girl. I'll be right down.

(He hangs up. His face becomes creased with grief which is unmistakably boyish. He straightens out, turns and goes)

CURTAIN

HARRY BIRD's office about an hour and a half later. The
place is dim now and almost desolate-looking. SAM comes
up the steps slowly and heavily. When he reaches the
level of the floor, he unscrews the cap of his bottle,
takes a good big swig, puts the cap back on the bottle,
puts the bottle back into his overcoat pocket, and looks
around the place. He turns on the pianola. He notices
the message on the blackboard, "Ave Maria," erases the
words. He goes to the water jar, moistens his handkerchief, touches it to his black eye, comes back to the slate
and wipes the whole thing with the wet handkerchief,
making it very clean. He takes up a piece of chalk and on
the slate prints in very large letters: I Am Sam. He then
signs this message, in handwriting, Sam. He looks at his
message a moment and then takes off his hat in a cheer
and waves it.

SAM

Hooray for Sam! Long live Sam! Vive la Sam!
        (He takes a swig)
Vive la Everybody! Vive la—YOU! Vive la—ME!
        (Pause, drunkenly)
Vive—vive!
        (He erases the slate with the wet handkerchief again,
        and in very large letters he prints)
V-I-V-E!
        (He turns off the pianola. A young man, about eighteen,
        scrambles up the steps into the office. SAM points to the
        blackboard)

69

You can see the message for yourself. What's the matter with you?

MESSENGER
(Breathless)
They said I'd find Mr. Hammer here—in Harry Bird's office.

SAM
Who are you?

MESSENGER
I'm one of the company messengers.

SAM
Yes, yes—but what's your name?
(He points to the blackboard)
Vive, vive!

MESSENGER
My name's Joe Rigga. I've got to find Mr. Hammer.
(He turns to go)

SAM
Wait a minute. What's the matter, boy?

MESSENGER
(Bitterly)
My best friend too. The best guy I ever met. The only writer who ever read one of my stories. But I'll show them. I'll be the same kind of writer he was. A great writer.

SAM
(Very quietly)
I'm drunk, see? I'm always drunk, but I get drunker when I get scared.
(He clutches the boy by the shoulders)
Joe—tell me what's happened. Tell me real quiet.

70

MESSENGER

I don't know for sure. They say he got killed—Harry Bird. They
say his car went over a cliff out in the valley. They—

SAM

Don't be silly, boy. Who says Harry Bird's been killed?

MESSENGER

Everybody—it's all over the place.

SAM

It's a lie.
>   (*He brings the bottle out and takes a swig*)
Harry Bird—killed! Nonsense.

MESSENGER

He was the only writer who ever talked to me. He was the only
one who asked me my name. Just because I'm a messenger *now*,
they think I'm going to be a messenger all the time.

SAM

>   (*Offering the bottle*)
He's *not* killed—you need a drink, that's all.

MESSENGER

No, I don't, but I'll take one anyway.
>   (*He takes the bottle, lifts it*)
Here's to—him. Gone—
>   (*He takes a swig*)
—but not forgotten.
>   (*He hands the bottle back to* SAM)

SAM

>   (*Lifting the bottle*)
Don't be silly.
>   (*He finishes what's in the bottle, looks around*)
Joe—it isn't going to make any difference, if it's true, but what
do they say happened?

71

MESSENGER

They say he was driving with a girl through the hills out in the valley—about a hundred miles an hour.
(*Pause*)
They went over the side, that's all.

SAM

They're a lot of little old women. A lot of shameless gossips.
(*Pointing to blackboard*)
Look at the message. Vive!

(BEN MANHEIM *comes running up the steps. He is breathless and excited*)

MANHEIM

Where's Mr. Hammer?

MESSENGER

I'm looking for him, too. They said he might be here.

MANHEIM

(*To* SAM)
He's been killed! He was going too fast!
(*To the* MESSENGER)
Well, go and find him. Go look for him. Look for him everywhere.
(MANHEIM *runs to the window and shouts*)
Patrick! Patrick!
(*Turns and sees the* MESSENGER, *almost pushes him*)
What are you waiting for? Go find him, boy.

MESSENGER

Where'll I go? Mr. Hammer can't bring him back to life, can he?

MANHEIM

(*Astounded*)
What's your name?

MESSENGER

My name is Joseph Rigga, and you can fire me. Go ahead, fire
me! He was my friend. He read my story, he talked to me, he
told me I could be a writer. Go ahead, fire me.

MANHEIM

(Gently, calming down)
You're not going to be fired.
(He sits down wearily)

MESSENGER

(Bitterly and a little ridiculously)
Yeah? Then I quit. I'm through with you—all of you. Three
years I've been a messenger, and not one of you would talk to
me. Not one of you would read my stories. He talked to me.
Why? Because he was a human being, not a piece of machinery.
To hell with all of you—you can keep your lousy money. I quit.
(He turns and runs down the steps. SAM looks around and
follows him)

MANHEIM

(Into telephone)
This is Ben Manheim. I'm in Harry Bird's office. If Mr. Ham-
mer is located, telephone me at this number, please.
(Pause, shouting)
Yes, I know what happened. I know all about it.
(Gently)
Thank you very much for wanting to tell me.
(He hangs up. HAMMER comes up the steps very slowly.
He looks at MANHEIM with terrible contempt)

HAMMER

Was that you shouting at me?

MANHEIM

Yes, it was, Patrick—

HAMMER
   (Furiously)
Well, you're fired, understand?

MANHEIM
   Very well, Patrick.

HAMMER
   How did you know where I was? You must be out of your head
to do a thing like that? What the hell's come over you? Shouting my name all over the place—my *first* name, as if I were
some punk around the place. Suppose somebody heard you?—
I've worked thirty-five years to build company discipline.
      (Mocking MANHEIM*)*
Patrick!—Patrick! Well, here I am. Now, what is it?

MANHEIM
   There's been an accident. We've been trying to reach you for
a half hour. Nobody has the slightest idea where you were.

HAMMER
   It so happens I was with Betty Fitch. I had to have a little talk
with her about the way she's been carrying on. Too much tem-
perament for a girl who isn't worth a nickel at the box-office
any more. I want her to be dropped. She's committed to one
more picture after *Danger Street*—that's the last.
      (Pause)
I was with *her*. My visit will save the company thousands of
dollars.

MANHEIM
   I understand, Patrick.

HAMMER
   Are you sure you do?

MANHEIM
   Yes, I am.

74

HAMMER

She's to be treated with the greatest delicacy. More parts are to be *discussed* with her—and greater parts. Then she is to be dropped.

MANHEIM

Yes, I know.

HAMMER

All right. Now, what is it you want to tell me?

MANHEIM

I thought it was going to be difficult for me to tell you this, but now I know it isn't.

HAMMER

Never mind—never mind. Just tell me.

MANHEIM

Harry Bird was killed in an automobile accident about an hour ago.

HAMMER

(*Furiously*)
That son of a bitch!
(*Swiftly*)
All right, get on the phone. What are we waiting for? Get the next best writer on the phone and let's fly him out here from New York—or wherever he is. Who's another writer who can do the story?

MANHEIM

(*Quietly*)
No writer can do it.

HAMMER

Don't talk like a fool, please. Writers are a dime a dozen. Rattle off some of their names. I'll pick one the way I pick horses. What are their names?

75

MANHEIM
John Donne, William Blake, Henry Thoreau—

HAMMER
Get Blake on the phone. He sounds like somebody who ought to be able to write. William Blake—that's a good solid name. Not like that Harry Bird. He did it on purpose. He wouldn't listen to me. He had to be a wise-guy, a guttersnipe. Had to run off and leave me holding the bag. I offered him money, but no, he wanted to rob me. So he went out and killed himself. So get William Blake on the phone.

MANHEIM
I'm sorry, Patrick—he's dead, too.

HAMMER
Dead? Who asked you to name dead writers? Get one of the other writers on the phone.

MANHEIM
They're *all* dead—

HAMMER
I want that story written, understand? I'm going to get it written.

MANHEIM
Excuse me, Patrick—why don't you forget it?

HAMMER
Why do you ask me to forget it?

MANHEIM
I ask you to forget it because it's an unholy, inhuman fantasy, born of hate.

HAMMER
Is it unholy for a man to hold fast to his faith?

76

MANHEIM

To faith founded on hate, it is. Forget it, Patrick.

HAMMER

I can see why you have never become a success. You have no
sense at all—no sense of the timely, no sense of the dramatic,
no sense of what people want and need. You're not a showman,
you're a book-reader.
(*Dramatically*)
When the world is full of death—when men are killing one
another—what do people think of? They think of Mother.
We'll have the biggest box-office hit in the history of pictures.
All we need is the story. The people are ready for it—they're
waiting for it—they're asking for it—they're praying for it. Get
me a writer on the phone and I'll talk to him myself. I'll pay
him five thousand a week. Get a man past thirty, but not past
forty—not too young, and not too old. Get a man I can talk to,
a man I can flatter, a man who can write but hasn't been around
too much. Get a man who has a little respect for money. Get
a man who won't push me around and then go out and kill himself. Get me a crook, but a little one.

MANHEIM

I could get a hundred writers, Patrick, but all of them put together couldn't do it. Ave Maria? Those aren't words, Patrick.
They go deep into the whole fable of human life.

HAMMER

The deeper the better. Get me a man who can write The
Bible. The world needs a new Bible.

MANHEIM

Only Saints can write a Bible. You're asking for too much.

HAMMER

I don't know why I have you around. There's no such thing as
asking for too much. The world hasn't come to an end just
because some guttersnipe of a writer has killed himself. To hell

77

with him. To hell with the story, too. If you say it can't be written, O.K., I believe you. Now, tell me what kind of a story will take advantage of the way the people of the world are feeling. We have a great responsibility to the people, Ben, and I for one don't intend to let them down. If you're the man I believe you are, you won't let them down, either. If my story is no good, all right, we'll forget it. We'll get another story.

(ROSE SCHORNBLOOM *comes in*)

(*Swiftly*)
Yes, Rose? What is it?

ROSE

I want to apologize for my behavior this afternoon, Mr. Hammer. I've been upset about my son, in the Army. I've come to finish my work. They told me I might find you here.

HAMMER

Oh, yes—it's all right, Rose. Don't feel bad. All of us get upset and unhappy once in a while. I've forgotten all about it.
(*He extends his hand.* ROSE *almost runs to him, kneels, and goes to work on the last three fingers of his left hand. He goes right on*)
Now, Ben, this is very important. We've got to have a great story, understand? We're turning out a lot of good pictures— the best ever made—but what we need is a great story, not just something run-of-the-mill.

(ROSE *is working away at his fingers now*)

Besides making money, we need a picture for prestige. We need something powerful, but tender too, with great understanding, with plenty of warmth—plenty of comedy—

(BEN MANHEIM *reaches out, as if seeking to interrupt the flow of words he can no longer tolerate*)

Now, don't interrupt, Ben. Hear me out. I'm not a reading-man. I don't know books. But I *do* know this business, and I

78

know what it needs. A great story—a story about the human struggle to live decently. This War is going to be over before we know it, and a new world is going to be made. We've got to be in on that—otherwise we're finished. Absolutely finished, Ben. Do you think I'd give that loud-mouth three weeks of my time if I didn't know which way the wind's blowing, and what we've got to do to stay alive in the world? We've got to have a whole new kind of writing, a whole new kind of pictures. We've got to make the world over. We've got to make life *itself* over—make it better, Ben.

MANHEIM

You can make the world over, Patrick. I'm sure you can. I know I can't. I've grown too fond of it, and too fond of life—the way it is—

HAMMER

You're not a business man, Ben. You're a dreamer.

HARRY'S VOICE

(Singing)
For an old man he is old—
And an old man he is gray
But a young man's heart is full of love
Get away, old man, get away.

HAMMER

(While HARRY sings)
Ben, you said the son of a bitch was killed! You've got to get these things straight!

(HARRY BIRD appears at the head of the stairs. His clothes are soiled and torn. He is smoking a cigarette. HAMMER gets up and moves toward him)

My boy, they told me you were dead.

HARRY

Who told you such a ridiculous thing?

79

HAMMER

Ben told me just a few minutes ago.

HARRY

    (To BEN*)*
What do you mean telling him I was dead?

BEN

I was told you were—

HARRY

Who told you?

BEN

Everybody said you'd been killed in an automobile accident.

HARRY

Well, I'm not dead, see? I was knocked out for a while, but I came out of it O.K.

    (A young DOCTOR *in a white uniform comes bouncing up the steps)*

I guess I almost died.

HAMMER

Doctor, how is he? Is he going to be all right?

DOCTOR

    (To HAMMER*)*
He was unconscious for an hour. We're not sure how serious the concussion is. He's got to come back to the hospital.

HAMMER

I thank God for this miracle.

    (He gets down on his knees, leaving his hand in the bowl of water)

I go down to my knees humbly and thank God for sparing your life.

HARRY
   Ah, get up off your knees.

HAMMER
      (Getting up)
   Doctor, see that he gets every attention—every attention! Have specialists fly out from New York.

DOCTOR
   We've got all the specialists we need at the hospital—

HAMMER
      (Realistically)
   What hospital is it?

DOCTOR
   The Good Samaritan.

HAMMER
   Ben, is that the best hospital?

MANHEIM
   They're all good.

HAMMER
      (Furious)
   Good isn't enough—I want the best.

DOCTOR
      (To HARRY)
   I can't allow you to stay here any longer.

HAMMER
      (Serious and powerful, to the DOCTOR)
   Just a moment, young man.
      (Tenderly)
   Harry—

DOCTOR

    (Almost angry)

He's been seriously injured—he's got to come back to the hospital.

HAMMER

    (To the DOCTOR*)*

I've been patient with you, young man, but I'm not going to be patient any longer. ·

DOCTOR

I'm responsible for your son.

HAMMER

My son?

    (Pause)

Don't think I haven't been watching you out of the corner of my eye, young man. Well, let me tell you something. I am the man who established the *Doctor Cavanaugh* pictures. I don't mind your wanting to make an impression on me, in the hope of leaving the Good Samaritan and joining my organization, but I will not allow you to interrupt me when—

DOCTOR

I don't know what you're talking about. Who the hell's Doctor Cavanaugh?

MANHEIM

This man doesn't want to be an actor.

HAMMER

Of course he does—he's been acting ever since he came here.

DOCTOR

    (Confused and angry)

I am a student specialist in the research of malignant tissue growths.

82

HAMMER
>   (*Shouting*)
You're an actor! How much are you paid for your work?

DOCTOR
I work under a research grant of the Good Samaritan Hospital.

HAMMER
I'll pay you five hundred dollars a week to start.

DOCTOR
>   (*To* HARRY)
I must ask you to come back to the hospital.

HAMMER
>   (*Very angry*)
Just a minute, young man. I'm offering you a chance to make a name for yourself. Five hundred a week to start, a hundred extra every six months until it's a thousand a week, and a seven-year contract after that. Ben, have Murphy draw up the papers.

MANHEIM
This man is not interested in moving pictures.

HAMMER
What do you mean?
>   (*To the* DOCTOR)
Is that true?

DOCTOR
I haven't the slightest idea what this is all about.

HAMMER
I'll give you an advance of five thousand dollars this afternoon.

DOCTOR
Five thousand dollars?

83

HAMMER

Ben, the next picture in our *Doctor Cavanaugh* series is to be about a young specialist in the research of—what was that, young man?

DOCTOR

Malignant tissue growths.

HAMMER

—Yes—whose salary is barely enough to make both ends meet. He's in love, but he can't get married because he can't afford it. He's offered a better job—of some sort—by somebody or other—put a good hack writer on the story—but he turns it down, so he can go on with his work. He loses his girl—she marries a very successful man—not a doctor—who is stricken a year later with some sort of tumor of the brain, and our boy is called in to investigate. Put two writers on it, and instruct them to keep our boy from getting the girl—but at the same time give the story a happy ending—the guy's happy in his work!
(*To the* DOCTOR)
Go over to my office and tell my secretary, Miss Henderson, I sent you there.

DOCTOR

Where is the office?

BEN

(*Taking the* DOCTOR *by the shoulders*)
Don't do it— Go back to the Good Samaritan Hospital.

DOCTOR

I could continue my research in the evenings.

HAMMER

You're an intelligent young man. Ask anybody how to get to Mr. Hammer's office. They'll tell you. Hurry, now.

(*The* DOCTOR *goes*)

84

MANHEIM

> (*Going with him*)

Listen to me, young man.

> (*They stand to one side, talking softly*)

HAMMER

> (*To* HARRY)

My boy, a few minutes ago when I heard the terrible news, I died. My own son was dead, gone from the world—forever. In my heart, I died, Harry. The great story he was to write was unwritten—and would never be written.

MANHEIM

> (*Turning*)

He doesn't want to be an actor.

HAMMER

> (*Almost shouting*)

Ben, I can't have you interfering in my affairs!

MANHEIM

This man's got important work to do.

DOCTOR

> (*To* HARRY)

We'd better go back now.

HARRY

> (*Gently*)

I don't like hospitals. You go back alone. I'm all right.

DOCTOR

> (*To* MANHEIM, *shaking his hand*)

Good-by, sir—and thanks very much.

> (*He turns to go*)

HAMMER

> (*To the* DOCTOR)

Just a minute, young man. I suppose you think you're being

85

very noble, going back to your work—well, you're not being noble, you're being a fool—but all right, I won't stop you. Go back to your little game of hide and seek. Spend your life looking for the cause of malignant tissue growths—but mark my words, you're headed for an empty life, because after you've discovered the cause, there isn't going to be anything you can do about it. Go back to your microscopes and knives and forks and teaspoons. I know the cause of more diseases than you'll ever hear about. Do you think you're going to keep people alive forever by finding out what causes death? You're going to shuttle back and forth between the known and the unknown and come up with ten cents' worth of information—THEY DIE! Well, I know they die. They begin to die the minute they're born, but while they're waiting, I give them escape. I give them beautiful dreams. I give them a church in which to worship grace and beauty. I give them anesthetics for their awful wounds. I give them laughter. Now get out! Don't take up any more of my time—you druggist!

(The DOCTOR goes in confusion. HAMMER turns to BEN)

I want you to get all the information you can about that fellow. The Doctor Cavanaugh pictures are out of style. We'll kill the whole series, and start a new one, with this boy, and a tougher villain than headaches, broken legs and appendicitis attacks—we'll go after the cause of things. Now, sit down, Ben—I want to talk to you.

MANHEIM

I'm sorry, Patrick, I must go now. I want to take a vacation.

HAMMER

(Shouting)

Sit down! We're on the threshold of a new day, and you want to go off like a hurt boy and pity yourself. How old do you think you are? You're three years younger than I am. Well, act your age. Where do you think the world would be if men ran away from their responsibilities just to be comfortable and happy?

86

(*Almost gently*)
Sit down, Ben.

> (BEN *sits down.* HAMMER *turns to* HARRY, *who is going through his desk, piling sheets of paper together—manuscripts, notes, and so on*)

How do you feel, my boy? Are you all right?

HARRY
I feel fine.

HAMMER
Are you sure you shouldn't go back to the hospital for a check-up?

HARRY
No, I feel fine. I feel like a new-born babe—twenty-seven years old. Even *you* look wonderful to me now, Old Man.

HAMMER
(*Pause*)
Harry, what are those papers?

HARRY
Nothing—idle notes—a couple of short stories—some scenes for a play. I thought I'd take 'em along—for reference.

HAMMER
I'd like to look at those notes, Harry.

HARRY
They're nothing—they wouldn't make sense to anybody but me.

HAMMER
You may have something there I could use. I've got a staff of fifty regular writers—a gang of thieves who sit around all day playing gin rummy, gossiping like a lot of old women, crying their eyes out because they aren't writing great books. Let me

87

put the whole mob of them to work. I'll hand every one of them a page of notes, and tell them to make a story out of whatever's on the page. I'll tell them to go to work or get out. How much do you want for the whole pile?

HARRY

No—it wouldn't do. The only thing written on this page is a name.

HAMMER

What is the name?

HARRY

(Holding the sheet)
Margaret Corrigan.

HAMMER

(Getting to his feet)
Where'd you get that name?

MANHEIM

I happened to mention it to him this afternoon.

HAMMER

Ben, for God's sake, why can't you follow instructions? I told you I didn't want that name bandied around. All day you've failed me—one thing after another. I've loved you like a brother—but how long do you expect me to endure these awful blunders?

HARRY

Ah, take it easy, Old Man. I won't mention the name to anybody as long as I live.
(He tears up the sheet of paper)
I've made a lot of trouble for you these three weeks. It's about time I got the hell out of here and let you alone. Ben is the best friend you've got.
(He offers his hand to HAMMER)
So long—Patrick Hammer.

88

HAMMER

   (*Takes his hand*)
My boy, where are you going?

HARRY

I'm going home. So long, Ben. I didn't mean to make any trouble.
   (*He turns to go*)

HAMMER

Harry, my boy! Don't go just yet. Wait a little longer. You've been here three weeks—stay a little longer.

HARRY

Somebody's waiting for me.

HAMMER

Harry, I've told Ben the story and I want to tell it to you, too.

HARRY

What story?

HAMMER

Ave Maria—our story, the story you're going to write for me.

HARRY

Listen, Old Man—I know Ave Maria is a great story—I'm not kidding—I speak humbly—it's great—but I can't write it. It's your story. I have enough trouble writing my own. Look at this bundle of notes. On every page I've tried to tell the truth—not about you, or Ben, or Miss Schornbloom—but about myself. But I haven't been able to do it. I get near the truth, but that's all. If I can't write the truth about myself, how can I write it about you?

HAMMER

You can, Harry—if any writer in the world can, you can. You've changed since your accident. You're not so bitter and angry.

Now, you can *really* write the story— Harry, please—I ask you—don't go off this way with nothing settled. Say you'll write the story.

HARRY

You're too great a man for me to figure out.

HAMMER

I'm *not* a great man, Harry. If you'll let me tell you the story you'll see that I'm not great—you'll see that no man is great. We don't count—you and I and the other fellow—we come and go, making noise, but we're nothing—nothing at all, Harry. Things count. *Things* are great, Harry—not us, not any of us.
(*He turns to* BEN)
We're all weak and foolish and full of terrible wounds. All of us together—the millions of us—are *almost* great—but not quite. We're ugly! We're made ugly by the trouble we're always having, and there's no beauty in us until we're hurt—until we've been made humble by failure—and then turn—each man in his own way—to the bright image of his childhood—the image of light and glory that fills his sleep as long as he lives. Sit down, Harry, and let me tell you the story.

HARRY

I've got to go. I'd write the story for you if I could, but I can't. I know I can't.
(*Pause*)
I'm sorry, Old Man. I'm really sorry.

HAMMER

(*Pause, softly*)
All right, Harry. Good-by, then, and God bless you.
(*Pause*)
Where's your girl? I want to give *her* my blessings, too.

HARRY

Thanks. She's at the bus station. We're going home to San Francisco to be married.

90

MANHEIM

Harry, you're not going to marry *that* girl?

HAMMER

(Angry)

Ben, will you shut up a minute?

(Gently)

My boy, I'm glad for you. I thank God for the girl. I know she'll make you very happy.

MANHEIM

(To HAMMER)

But you don't understand.

HAMMER

(Angrier)

Ben, will you please shut up?

(To HARRY)

My boy, can I help you?

HARRY

No—thanks a lot, Old Man.

HAMMER

A little present, Harry. I'll get Murphy to write out a check for twenty-five thousand dollars. You can pay me back when you feel like it. No strings attached— I swear to God I'm telling the truth.

HARRY

So long, Old Man.

(He begins to go)

MANHEIM

Harry—as one who's admired your writing—I ask you with all my heart not to marry that girl.

(The door opens)

You've had an accident. Something's happened to you. You don't know what you're doing.

(MARTHA *comes in*)

HARRY

I know what I'm doing, Ben.
(*He turns to* MARTHA, *smiling*)
O.K., Martha. I've got everything.

MANHEIM

I must talk to you, young woman.

HARRY

It's all right, Ben.

MARTHA

(*To* HARRY)
Your friend Sam's downstairs—drunk. He's lying in the street. I tried to help him up, but I couldn't.

(HARRY, *forgetting himself, turns quickly and goes down the stairs, leaving* MARTHA *standing in front of* MANHEIM. *She moves imperceptibly to follow* HARRY, *but can't.* MANHEIM *stares at* MARTHA. *She looks as if she might burst into tears. There is a moment of awkwardness. Suddenly she turns and runs to the stairs, to go*)

MANHEIM

(*Powerfully*)
Just a minute, please.

(MARTHA *stops*)

I want to talk to you.

(MARTHA *turns—frightened and troubled.* HAMMER *watches, looking from* MARTHA *to* MANHEIM)

Please come here.

92

(As if hypnotized MARTHA moves to MANHEIM. He looks her straight in the eye)

This afternoon I thought I knew the truth about you. I thought you were acting, but now I'm not so sure. I don't believe you yourself meant to become the person you *have* become to Harry Bird. To a simpler person you would be what you are, and you know what that is—the good Lord knows I don't. Harry Bird is a writer. He has *created* the person he *wants* you to be. You may be an actress, but I don't think you could go on acting that part for the rest of your life. Now, I may be wrong, and I hope I am. Only you know—nobody else. If I'm right, I ask you to go away—leave him alone. Let things quiet down, then come to me. I promise to see that you get a contract.

(Deeply hurt and stunned, almost in tears, MARTHA turns and runs down the stairs)

HAMMER

What the hell do you think you're doing, Ben?

MANHEIM

You don't understand. I *had* to tell her. It hurt me to do it—and I hope I'm wrong—but I had to do it.

HAMMER

Why?

MANHEIM

I'm afraid she's a cheap little ambitious whore.

HAMMER

Who said so?

MANHEIM

She did—she said so herself. He asked her, and she told him. I thought she was acting, but I'm afraid she wasn't. And then for some reason, he liked her and *made* her over, the way he wanted her to be—the way she *seems* to be.

93

HAMMER

(*Quietly*)

You've never learned much from the books you've read, have you? Let's say you're right. Do you think I give a good God damn what she is? If he likes her and takes her home, he'll write the story. I know he will. When are you going to start understanding things? Now she'll go off and cry and never see him again—and then where am I? Right back where I started, with the story as far from being written as ever. I know he meant to go home and write the story—I know it. And now, just because you had to shoot off your big loud mouth, she's run off, broken-hearted. Well, I tell you that son of a bitch won't write another word until he's found her—and if he doesn't find her, he'll think he's lost the only woman in the world for him. When are you going to stop being a fool? Now go out and find her and bring her back—do you hear? You drove her away, so go bring her back.

MANHEIM

(*Standing, pleading, deeply troubled*)

I'm tired, Patrick. Maybe I was wrong. If I was, they'll find each other. I can't do another thing. I want to go home.

HAMMER

(*Shouting*)

Go out and find her—bring her back!

(MANHEIM *goes.* HAMMER *turns to* ROSE. *He speaks gently*)

Rose. You saw that girl. Is she a whore?

ROSE

Can a woman who loves a man that way be a whore?

HAMMER

Has she been a whore?

ROSE

Is there any woman who hasn't?

94

HAMMER
(*Amazed*)
You have never spoken this way before.

ROSE
There hasn't been anyone to speak to.

HAMMER
I've known you eleven years.

ROSE
But you have never before been who you are today—and I have
not been who I am. We are made by one another. We are not
made in the woman's belly, but in the world's. We are one or
another of the nine months which shall some day be the birth
of the real human race. If my poor son in the Army is killed,
how can he help the infant to be born?

HAMMER
I'm amazed.
(*Looking at hands*)
Are you finished?

ROSE
I have been finished for some time.

HAMMER
Then why didn't you go?

ROSE
I have listened many times to you and Mr. Manheim and your
writers talking about stories, and I have always felt that something was wrong with them. Please—Mr. Hammer—this once,
let me stay. I won't be noticed. I'll pretend to be working.

HAMMER
I'm amazed!

(*The downstairs door opens.* HAMMER *extends his hand
to* ROSE, *who takes it*)

95

ROSE

Thank you, Mr. Hammer.

(HARRY BIRD *comes in supporting* SAM, *who is still pretty drunk*)

SAM

The dirty little gossips told me you were dead! I didn't believe them, but I got drunk just in case it was true.

HARRY

Here—lie down on this couch.

(SAM *lies down*)

SAM

Vive! vive! vive!
(*He goes to sleep*)

HARRY

(*He looks around*)
Where is she?

HAMMER

She'll be back in a minute, Harry. I told her I had to talk over a few things with you, so she went out for a walk.

HARRY

What the hell did you tell her that for?

HAMMER

Harry—while you were gone—I had a chance to get a little acquainted with her. She's the girl for you. She's as beautiful as a girl I once knew in Dublin. She loves you. I thank God that you've found her—that you're going to marry her—because I know what it is to go through life with everything the next best, instead of the best.

(*The telephone rings.* HAMMER *answers it*)

Yes?
> (*Pause*)

Yes, Ben?
> (*He listens*)

Bring her back, that's all—
> (*Shouting*)

Just bring her back!
> (*He listens*)

All right, then—keep her there. I'll send him to her.
> (*He hangs up*)

Harry, you've got to hurry. She's in the bus station. She's bought a ticket to Great Falls. The bus is leaving in ten minutes.

HARRY
> (*Stunned*)

Great Falls? Who the hell are you talking about?

HAMMER

Your girl—the girl you're going to marry. She wants to go home to Great Falls. Don't let her do it. Take her to San Francisco. She's yours, my boy—don't let her get away. Don't lose her. I know what it is to lose the only person in the world who can keep love alive.

HARRY
> (*Shouting*)

Home in Great Falls? You're crazy! She's never been in Great Falls in her life. She invented that story.

> (*The telephone rings.* HAMMER *answers it*)

HAMMER
Yes?
> (*He listens*)

Yes, he's here.

HARRY
> (*Excited*)

Who is it?

97

HAMMER

 (*Into telephone*)
I can't hear you. Please speak a little louder.
 (HAMMER *listens*)

HARRY

What's the matter?

HAMMER

 (*Into telephone*)
I think you'd better talk to *him*.
 (*To* HARRY)
She wants me to tell you something, but I can't make out what
it is. She's crying.

HARRY

Who's crying, for God's sake?

HAMMER

Your girl, Harry. Talk to her. She's a little upset, that's all. It's
nothing. Be gentle and kind—be patient.

HARRY

 (*Confused, scared and not sure he ought to go to the
 telephone*)
What the hell's she crying for? What's she want to talk to me
by telephone for?

HAMMER

Talk to her, my boy—it's nothing. She's the best—she's yours—
don't lose her.

HARRY

 (*Goes to the telephone, looks at it, takes it up slowly.
 He speaks softly, almost whispering*)
Martha?
 (*He listens. The expression of ·pain on his face changes
 to an expression of relief and delight and tender regard.*

98

He is almost laughing and crying at the same time when
he speaks)

Ah, now, Martha—you don't have to cry about *that*. I didn't
mean to leave you that way.

(Softly, gently)

Now, stop your crying, do you hear? Stop your crying. I'm
sorry. I just didn't want to see Sam drunk, that's all.

(He listens)

He's all right now. He's gone to sleep.

(Pause, he listens, then speaks softly)

Martha? What's this about Great Falls?

(He listens, speaks with relief)

For the love of Mike, Martha, stop acting for Ben Manheim—
you're wrecking his faith.

(He laughs)

Tell him to go home, and you wait there for me. We'll catch
the next bus—there's no hurry. I'll be there in a few minutes.

(Listens)

Of course I'm not angry—I was just a little scared, that's all.

(Listens)

O.K.

*(He hangs up. He stands a moment, dazed with relief.
He looks at* HAMMER, *and nods. He looks at* ROSE
SCHORNBLOOM, *and nods, smiling)*

She's mine.

(Whispering)

She's always been mine. She saved my ridiculous life. After the
accident I dreamed I was going to die, and I didn't care. Why
not die? It was all nonsense—loneliness and noise and running
about, anyway. Why not be done with it? For God's sake—how
clean do you want your hands to be? Then in my dream came
a beautiful blinding light—I opened my eyes and there before
me, behold, was the face of love and truth and beauty—her
face—and I cared a lot. I kept caring for what seemed centuries,
living my poor life again and again, struggling with everything
for another chance—struggling to be born again, and then at last
it happened, I got my chance, and I opened my eyes. There

99

before me again, looking into mine, were the eyes of my love, filled with tears. I got up to take her home with me.
> (*He kisses* ROSE SCHORNBLOOM *on the forehead*)

Good-by, Rose Schornbloom.

HAMMER
> (*On his knees*)

I thank God, my boy, for sparing your life.

HARRY

So long, Old Man.
> (*He turns and runs out of the place, with* HAMMER *shouting after him*)

HAMMER
> (*Shouting*)

Write the story, my boy! Now, you can write it! Write our story, Harry!

> (*The downstairs door slams,* HAMMER *runs to the window*)

Harry—my boy—I'll send Murphy up to San Francisco with a contract and a check—you'll need money for a new house—for clothes for your wife and your children.

HARRY'S VOICE
> (*Shouting*)

Go home, Old Man—go home.

HAMMER
> (*Shouting*)

My boy—tell me you'll write the story.

HARRY'S VOICE

I'll try, Old Man. I give you my word—I'll try!

HAMMER
> (*Shouting*)

I thank God. That's all I ask, Harry. Go home with your girl, and God bless you.

> (*He returns to* ROSE *who's been packing up her things, and is now ready to go. He sits down and cries audibly*)

ROSE

What's the matter, Mr. Hammer?

HAMMER

I'm old, Rose. And the world's so young.

> (*He dials a number on the telephone, and with tears streaming down his face he speaks forcefully*)

Murphy? Mr. Hammer.

> (*He turns to* ROSE, *putting his hand over the telephone*)

You can go now, Rose. Thank you very much.

> (ROSE *goes.* HAMMER *returns to the telephone*)

Now, listen, Murphy—listen carefully. The son of a bitch is going to write the story. It took me three weeks to do it, but I finally did it. Now, listen. He's on his way to the bus station to pick up one of our extras—a girl named Martha Harper. He's going to marry her. He's never met you, so I want you to get on that bus. I want you to strike up an acquaintance with him— tell him you're a lawyer or something—but you've read his books—every one of them. You have, haven't you? All but the first two? O.K., talk about the books you've read. He'll talk to you. Now, listen, Murphy. I want you to find out how little he'll take for the story after he's written it. I think we can get it for almost nothing. I want you to find out what he thinks of me, too. Tell him you met me once in connection with some legal work and that you think I'm—well, tell him you think I'm a crook. Put it in those words, do you understand? And then listen very carefully to what he tells you. When you get to San Francisco telephone me. Have you got it?

> (*Pause*)

O.K.

> (*He hangs up. He talks to himself, while he dials another number*)

The son of a bitch—trying to pull a fast one on me!
(*Into telephone*)
This is Patrick Hammer. Let me speak to Miss Corrigan,
please.
(*He waits*)
Margaret, I've got good news for you. I've found the story with
which to introduce you to the American public at last.

(*The downstairs door opens*)

Is it a good story? It's going to be the biggest picture I've ever
made. Now, I've canceled all engagements for the evening. I'll
come by in a half hour and pick you up. We'll drive out to my
place and spend the night there, and I'll tell you all about it.

(BETTY FITCH *has stood at the head of the stairs, listen-
ing to the last few sentences*)

Yes—in a half hour.
(*He hangs up*)

BETTY

Listen, you old wreck, what are you trying to do, give me the
bum's rush? You're not going to make a fool out of me, you
horrible old man.

HAMMER
(*Powerfully*)
Behave yourself, young woman. You must be dreaming.
(*He is about to go*)

BETTY
(*Screaming*)
I suppose I was dreaming this afternoon when you were in my
dressing room?

HAMMER
(*Going*)
Oh, don't be ugly.
(*He goes*)

BETTY

Who made me ugly? You did—you, with your soft fat body.
(*She sits down on the couch where* SAM's *sleeping.* SAM
sits up)

SAM

Ah, come on—don't cry. You're all right.
(*He gets up and turns on the pianola*)
Come on, don't cry. You're beautiful! You're wonderful! Come
on—dance with me!

(*She gets up, sobbing, and they begin to dance*)

BETTY

(*Blubbering*)
I'm alone—I've got no friend in the world.

SAM

No? You've got me, honey.

(*The curtain begins to come down*)

And I've got you, and we've both got a lot of time. Vive!—
Vive!

THE CURTAIN IS DOWN